The Woman Sealed in the Tower

. . . being a view of feminine spirituality
as revealed by the legend of Saint Barbara

Betsy Caprio

PAULIST PRESS
New York/Ramsey

Illustrated and Designed by
Gloria Claudia Ortíz

Library of Congress
Catalog Card Number:
82-83983

ISBN:
0-8091-2486-6

Published by Paulist Press
545 Island Road, Ramsey, N.J. 07446

Printed and bound in the
United States of America

Contents

To one who came in the name of the Lord

Introduction

ONE WINTER MORNING, seven women sat in a warm New England living room, together for a session of their study group known as Centerpoint.[1] (Their friends and children and husbands kept getting the name wrong, thinking it was "Centerpiece" or "Needlepoint," joking that these were more appropriate labels for a women's gathering.)

On this snowy day, they deviated from the prepared text and began to explore the four elements of ancient times—earth, air, water, fire—and the simple ways each was present in their lives. "Earth surely is part of my world," said a mother of six, whose children tracked mud into their kitchen daily. Another gardened, several raised beautiful indoor plants, all waged battle against dust and grime. Earthwomen. From there they went on to themselves as air-women (". . . when I rise above it all," said one), then water-women and fire-women (". . . that's the flame inside that keeps me caring," said another). They had the hunch that they were using another language for what C. G. Jung has described as the four functions of the psyche: sensation, thinking, feeling and intuition.

I was part of that Centerpoint group in Massachusetts' Berkshire Hills. Two and a half years later, I found myself living in southern California, far from these dear friends but still tuned to our explorations of the earth and air and water and fire within and without. Their prayers and letters sustained me; I shared my experiences and reflections with them.

At the same time, I was trying to put together ideas for an introductory book on feminine spirituality—and I wanted to find a woman's story to use as a loose framework. Robert Johnson has already written the small and beautiful volume *She*,[2] which has become a prototype of this style. In it, he uses the myth of ancient Greece's Psyche as a vehicle for examining the individuation process in women. Erich Neumann has left us a more scholarly treatment of the same tale.[3] And Rosemary Haughton has done something similar with Mary's story in her *Feminine Spirituality: Reflections on the Mysteries of the Rosary*.[4] Somehow, I felt there was still another woman's tale which could speak about the work on the elements my friends and I had done . . . but which story? where to find it?

I searched Scripture, but nothing connected for me. I thought of analyzing a modern day tale, as Ann Ulanov has done with Dorothy of Oz[5] and Barbara Hannah has with the heroine of *Wuthering Heights,* Emily Brontë's Cathy.[6]

I turned to fairy tales, to legends of the Greeks and stories of the native Americans, and finally came full circle to an old love, the lives of the saints.[7] Among these, one Easter morning, there appeared the legend of the early Christian martyr Saint Barbara. And here was my story, for Barbara not only develops as a woman, but lives out—as my friends and I felt ourselves doing—earth-woman, air-woman, water-woman and fire-woman.

An old book I had read from to my daughters, years earlier, gave me an elaborated version of Barbara's life and death.[8] At the end of this retelling of her legend by the British author was the line, ". . . St. Barbara's special day is December 4th, and lots of people's birthdays are on that day, and there is a town in America called after her."

And there was a synchronistic "click" as I remembered that just the week before a special friend had said, "You must explore Santa Barbara"—meaning the beautiful southern California city of that name. It seemed a verification of my choice of Barbara's tale. No sooner had I begun work on a first draft of this book than I learned that the same friend's birthday was Saint Barbara's day. It seemed a double confirmation of my choice; there are no accidents. The book is dedicated to this dear person, who was also on the scene the first time I tried to share some of these ideas with a class. I've really been so richly blessed in those sent to help me see and love and learn.

Soon after this, I made a pilgrimage with another woman to the famous Mission Santa Barbara, a couple of hours' drive from my home in Los Angeles. The beautiful old church, known as "The Queen of the Missions," was dedicated on December 4, 1786. It is all pink and cream-colored stone, and over the doors is a carved Barbara, the tower that is her emblem at her side. In various spots—over the altar, by the entrance—is the image of the rising sun: rebirth, new life, light after the dark night. Santa Barbara is the seventh in the famous chain of missions established by the Franciscans in early California, and it is an active parish to this day. I loved the whole place, drew closer to the long-dead (perhaps even imaginary) woman for whom it was named, asked her for insight, and set to work. The result is this small book. It is a very personal—even fanciful—interpretation of Barbara's tale, not meant as the only way to view the legend; I offer it as an example of what it means to reflect on one's own story, hoping the reader will be given some food for thought about her (or his) personal mythology.

Here are the names of those women whose lovely feminine qualities have been seed for me and whom I want to thank publicly: my beautiful daughters Cecelia and

Julia; from the Massachusetts Centerpoint group, Teresa Giardina De Cesare, Ann McGaharn, Elna Nugent, Beverley O'Brien, Barbara Rupprecht, Gwen Sears, Kathy Wright and, especially, Bannie Giovanetti, whose journal reflections on the four elements in her life are found with the experiments in the appendix; and these women of California who have been a support and helped to illuminate the subject of feminine spirituality: Diana Brennan, Rita Brown, Kathie Busch, C. S. J., Ronda Chervin, Ruth Cron, Joy Daly, Ruth Edwards, S. N. D., Gemma Fisher, S. N. J. M., Marita Goodwin (fellow pilgrimess to Santa Barbara), Laura Gormley, S. S. L., Jill Halverson, Luanne Lynch, Carole Coleman Michelson, Mary Betten Mitchell, Maxine Stephen, and Claire Ocksner and Lore Zeller of the C. G. Jung Institute of Los Angeles, as well as Saint Barbara herself, who qualifies as a California woman by adoption. Thanks too to patient editor Jean Marie Hiesberger.

Two men must be thanked also. One is Meredith Mitchell of Los Angeles, Jungian analyst and teller of fairy tales, the other is Jack Sanford of San Diego, whose work has been a touchstone for myself and so many others. Both have read and provided many helpful lights on *The Woman Sealed in the Tower,* as well as their encouragement and support.

May Saint Barbara send all these friends an extra measure of her "tower power."

Easter 1981
Manhattan Beach, California

---

1. Centerpoint is a four-year series of group sessions focusing on the psychology of Jung, originally from the (Episcopal) Education Center in St. Louis. Information available now from Centerpoint, 22 Concord St., Nashua, NH 03060.

2. Robert Johnson, *She* (New York: Perennial Library, 1977).

3. Erich Neumann, *Amor and Psyche* (Princeton: Princeton University Press, 1971).

4. Rosemary Haughton, *Feminine Spirituality* (New York: Paulist Press, 1976).

5. Ann Bedford Ulanov, *The Feminine in Jungian Psychology and in Christian Theology* (Evanston, IL: Northwestern University Press, 1971), Chapter 12.

6. Barbara Hannah, *Striving Towards Wholeness* (New York: G. P. Putnam's Sons, 1971).

7. A notable addition to hagiography is the work of Marie-Louise von Franz, who has interpreted the visions and dreams of saints from the psychological viewpoint. See her *The Passion of Perpetua* (Irving, Texas: Spring Publications, Inc., 1980; originally published in 1949), and *The Dreams and Visions of St. Niklaus von der Flüe* (Irving, Texas: Spring Publications, Inc., 1981; privately published in 1959).

8. Joan Windham, *Sixty Saints for Girls* (New York: Sheed and Ward, 1962. Reprinted in *Story Library of the Saints,* London: Harwin Press, Ltd., 1974).

I Saint Barbara's Story

" "O NCE UPON A TIME . . ." our fairy tales start—and some of these fairy tales even have dim connections to a real time and to real people.

The story of Saint Barbara of Heliopolis is such a fairy tale, woven throughout the first fourteen centuries of Christendom by storytellers drawn to vague memories of a young woman martyred in post-apostolic days. Very little that we could call history is known about Barbara—but that is not the point. What does matter is the pious romance that grew up around her and was spread and elaborated on throughout the Christian world, so much so that by the ninth century devotion to Saint Barbara had reached cultic proportions.

Stories don't live accidentally. And, especially, they do not flourish for hundreds of years by accident. Stories are kept alive when people somehow find their lives mirrored in them. What is it in Barbara's story that spoke to the peasants and monks and nuns and royalty of medieval Europe? And is it possible that a story with such a long life in the past could have sprung so deeply from that subterranean story level of us all that it may still speak to twentieth century story-lovers?

Here is the fairy tale version of Saint Barbara's life, culled from several sources (and with dialogue and scenery and emotion added in the manner allowed storytellers of all times).

The Legend of Saint Barbara

Once upon a time there was a young woman named Barbara. She and her father
Dioscorus were pagans, and her father had two causes of concern about his daughter. One
was that she would meet Christians, and the other was that some man would want to
marry her. Barbara was very beautiful, and her father was most proud of her and wanted
to keep her to himself.

Dioscorus decided to build a high tower, one with only two windows at the top. He said
to himself, "If I put Barbara in this tower and seal it up, no one will ever be able to see
her beauty or speak to her about this religion called Christianity." And so Dioscorus built
the tower and surrounded it with beautiful gardens, and when he had finished it he called
Barbara to him and asked her to step inside. She did, and before she could turn around,
Dioscorus had closed up the entrance to the tower and sealed it over, leaving his daughter
all alone in the dark.

Now the only connection with the outside world which Barbara had been left was a
basket tied to a rope. She could lower this from one of the two tower windows with her
empty dishes and her laundry, and the serving women of her father's household would
outfit it with food and clean clothing for her to draw back up.

Barbara gradually grew used to her tower. And one day, due to the kindness of a local
Christian who had taken pity on the imprisoned pagan girl, she found a book in her
basket. Now Barbara could read—and what she read amazed her, for the book was about
Jesus' living and dying and returning to life. Barbara read the book over and over with
fascination, and finally dared to write a note saying she wanted to learn more about

Christianity. She slipped the note into her basket, among the dishes and clothing, and lowered it down.

Somehow—we do not know just how—a priest was sent to her. (Perhaps he was transported to the tower miraculously, or—some say—her father was told that Barbara needed a doctor, and did not know enough to question the man who came along and said he **was** *a doctor . . . of the soul, of course.) In any event, Barbara was instructed in Christianity, and one day in her tower she was baptized.*

Now there came a time when Dioscorus had to be away, and Barbara instructed the workmen on his land to climb up and chop a third window in her tower. She was, after all, the daughter of their employer, so the workmen obeyed her, and when her father came home he looked up and saw the tower with three windows in it. "What is this?" he roared. Barbara leaned out of the new window and said, "I have added a third window, father, so that I can always have a reminder of the Holy Trinity."

Dioscorus was furious, for he knew now that Barbara had become a Christian. He flew into a rage, broke open the sealed-off doorway, ran up the steps to the top of the tower and flung Barbara out of the window by her long hair. But Barbara's guardian angel protected her, depositing her safely in a ravine in the thick wood nearby.

Barbara lived in the woods. One day, her father (who had been hunting for her ceaselessly) tracked her down. He dragged her before a local magistrate named Marcian and angrily said to her, "Renounce your God and your faith by offering a sacrifice to our gods, or die!" Barbara told her father she would not do this because she had pledged herself to Jesus, and although Dioscorus tore her flesh with iron hooks and beat her with rods at the order of the judge, she would not change her answer. He brought a rope to hang her, but it turned into a belt. He even lit a fire to burn her, but the fire turned into clay.

Finally, the cruel father wrapped his daughter's long hair around one hand and, with his sword clutched in the other, dragged her off to the top of a nearby mountain. Barbara prayed for strength, and at the moment her father severed her head from her body, she was caught up in a vision of Jesus, her Lord and love.

Now, Dioscorus turned to go back down the mountain, and as he did so a tremendous thunderstorm with lightning broke loose, and he was struck and killed by a fiery bolt.

The End

This legend, which was especially popular in Germany, seems to have been an early version of what we recognize as the story of Rapunzel. In the Grimm Brothers' versions of that later fairy tale there are many of the Saint Barbara ingredients: the beauty of the young girl, her betrayal by her father, the tower in which she is imprisoned, her communication with the outside world by something lowered from a tower window (in Rapunzel's case, of course, her long hair—another Barbara feature), the man who comes to the tower with a message of love, the defiance of the young woman in the cause of this love, her antagonist (not father, but witch) who attacks by mutilating her hair and then sends her away to "a waste and dreary place," the continuing faith of the heroine, and the happy ending of union with the beloved (the Rapunzel fairy tale, in a late version, reads, "Then he took her to his kingdom, where they were received with great joy—and there they lived long and happily").[1]

Did any of the Barbara/Rapunzel incidents really happen? The historian is concerned with such questions, but the explorer of the human soul need only be aware of the powerful attraction of Barbara's tale, its inner reality rather than its external factuality.

We find ourselves, as was mentioned earlier, in our favorite stories. We bring who we are and where we are to these tales and are drawn to those (old stories, new stories, movie and TV stories) which seem to speak about what's happening within us at the moment. This writer has been attracted to the legend of Saint Barbara because it seems, for her, a lovely reflector of her very present concern with the spiritual growth of women—and that is how the tale will be explored in the following chapters. Others, of course, might find Barbara's story a carrier of *their* immediate concerns; it could be read as being about the role of women in society or in the Church, or it could be about fathers and daughters, or even seen as a tale about the development of the feminine side of a man's personality.

But, for now, let's look at Barbara and her legend as, somehow, typical of what goes on in many women as their spiritual lives unfold. Perhaps she was kept alive by our sisters of long ago because her story spoke so powerfully of just this.[2]

1. An even earlier maiden-in-the tower story is the Greek myth of Danaë and Zeus. Danaë's father, like Barbara's, locked her up so she would see no men. Stith Thompson's *Motif-Index of Folk-Literature* (Bloomington: Indiana University Press, 1955) gives us an idea of the many cultures which have used this theme (see Vol. 5, section T381ff.) and in *Once Upon a Time: On the Nature of Fairy Tales* (Bloomington: Indiana University Press, 1976), Max Lüthi traces the origins of *Rapunzel*.

2. In *The Woman's Tale* (New York: Seabury Press, 1980), Ronda Chervin and Mary Neill find themselves—and invite the reader to do the same—in *Rapunzel* and eleven other tales and legends.

II Barbara Is Sealed in the Tower

Earth

SAINT BARBARA'S LEGEND is set in the magic land of fairy tales, over the rainbow or, maybe, east of the sun and west of the moon. (G. K. Chesterton, in *The Ballad of St. Barbara*, has her in "the desolate golden lands.")[1] The hints of history place her, variously, as having lived—if, indeed, she ever did live—in Heliopolis in lower Egypt or in Antioch, sometimes in Rome or Tuscany or Nicomedia, and the dates for her life are given as being between 235 and 313 A.D. The where and when of our story are not as important to us, however, as the what.

When her tale begins, Barbara and her father are the only characters. There is no mother. There are no sisters, no brothers—just a beautiful young woman and her possessive, even jealous, father, who is on guard that Barbara meet neither men nor Christians. Barbara, apparently, has no older woman around to model for her a conscious feminine way of engaging the world. What's more, she seems to have little or no sense of the "-ness" of Barbara. She is like our own young daughters or nieces or students, like ourselves before we knew we were Ruth or Teresa or Marita.

And Barbara's father builds a tower to imprison her, to keep her in this undeveloped state. We can almost see him ordering the workmen to bring the bricks or stones, to spread the mortar, to leave just two small windows at the top of the tower (his measure of charity to his daughter). The tower is finished and the father asks Barbara to step inside, just as the witch in *Hansel and Gretel* invites the young girl to step into her oven. Barbara, not as self-possessed as Gretel, obeys meekly. She participates in her own imprisonment without question, the story says.

What must have been in Barbara's heart and mind when her father led her into this prison and sealed her away? What would we have felt in her place—or, have we been there too? Have we, like Barbara, had our selves sealed off and not known it was happening? Perhaps we even helped to lay the bricks and spread the mortar for our own towers, then sank helplessly to the packed-down earth at the bottom of them. Perhaps Barbara—or we—thought she deserved such treatment, was not worthy of better.

And yet, there may be a time for tower-living. What looks like a prison of invisibility can also be an island of safety, a place of such simplicity that we are forced to develop our own inner resources for lack of outer ones. The tower gives us time, and it gives us perimeters. We might wonder whether Barbara, had she led a normal life and settled into typical medieval housewifery, would have missed the experience of being tested so.

It seems part of human (and animal) nature to find a space set apart for oneself. We talk about having a home of our own, or even a room or a corner of our own. This hunger needs to be honored. It is about the desire to experience externally what we are called to within: the awareness of our singularity.[2] The desire for a place set apart (or a *temenos,* a sanctuary) is a manifestation of the call to individuality or individuation.

There are women, and men, who recognize this call and set out to provide space for it. Still others, like Barbara, have the tower experience forced on them, often thinking they would have it almost any other way—then look back later to discover it was in their days as tower-dweller that their interior lives began to unfold. A great many of us, however, neither seeking our own spot for growth nor having it imposed upon us, bypass our opportunities for incubation.

The irony of Barbara's story is that her father, in his efforts to stifle his daughter's life, does just the opposite. He isolates her in a dwelling shaped like the earliest image of psychological and spiritual wholeness (the circle or the square),[3] strips her of all distractions so that she has no choice but to confront her own nature, and thereby inadvertently sets in motion the process which will lead to both faith and love for Barbara—and death for himself. Even more, the father surrounds his prisoner daughter with another image of the growth that lies ahead for her: the "marvelous gardens," a sign of feminine beauty and fruition. (He is what is called, in India, an unconscious ally.)

We have each had such allies, each had tower opportunities offered or thrust upon us. Barbara, as we shall see, uses hers well. This limited young girl, forced and sealed into a dark cage by one she might have hoped would protect her, has within her the potentialities she needs to become victorious *Saint* Barbara by the end of her story.

One way of describing the potentialities in each of us is to picture them with symbols. The ancients, for example, as well as the Church in medieval times, spoke of four elements that made up all of creation (including the human body): Earth, Air, Water and Fire. This foursome is especially appropriate as a representation of four functions in our personalities.[4] One reason, in fact, for the continuing appeal of astrology through the ages has been that people found themselves described—somehow—by the symbols of earth, air, water and fire.

Barbara's story can be divided into quadrants, one for her cultivation of each of these elements. At the end of it, we will see them fit together into a whole, like pieces of a pie cut into quarters. She will evolve into that wholeness for which her tower stands. (Four is, some say,[5] the number of psychological and spiritual wholeness. For example, the cross with its four arms is a pre-Christian symbol of totality, and Scripture is larded with foursomes that speak to us of all things coming together: the garden of Eden with its four rivers at the four compass points, the four corners and four winds of the earth of Revelation, the four-walled, twelve-gated new Jerusalem.)

This first part of Barbara's life has her very much in touch with the element of earth. Putty in her father's hands, she is encased in a container made of earth—perhaps bricks of clay made on his land, or rocks and stones from the ground around, all held together by more dried earth. The tower would have been dark and damp at the bottom, with just enough light from the two windows above to show her the stairs to the upper level. For all Barbara knows, this is to be her home for the rest of her life; she must come to terms with it.

A woman needs to develop her earth qualities, that at-homeness with matter and her surroundings that enables her to see what is there and what must be taken care of. Sometimes this is called the sensation function in our personalities. The serving women who receive Barbara's dishes and laundry probably have this earth-ness working for them. In fact, women who care for others, as mothers and nurses and teachers and social workers, often earn themselves the title of Earth Mother, so good are they at tending to material things.

We need the grounding quality of earth, need to "come down to earth," be at home with our senses and our bodies—in a word, earthy. This quality in a woman, well-developed, can nurture and provide stable, solid ground for herself and for others, just as good soil does. The woman with her earth-nature in play can be fertile, bear fruit. And when she has rooted herself well, her other attributes will bud organically, from within, in the most natural of ways.

Without an earth side to ourselves, however, we are unrooted, easily uprooted, undernourished and even barren. Without earth, we can't nurture the seeds sent our way; we will be neglectful of our mothering of others—and of ourselves. Too little earth in us can lead to our devaluing the importance of the material and, especially, discounting the environment in which we live.

But sometimes we go overboard in our earth-ness, and it can make us heavy, plodding, earthbound. That's when we smother those near to us, just as a seed planted too deep is buried by the earth. The woman with too much earth in her make-up can become the Terrible, Devouring Mother.

"Barbara gradually grew used to her tower," the legend tells us. This place which became her home was where she learned of her earth qualities, and where she learned of her life's work. Prison?—or sacred vessel?

1. *The Ballad of St. Barbara* in *Collected Poems,* G. K. Chesterton (New York: Dodd, Mead and Co., 1932).

2. M. Esther Harding elaborates on the use of the word "virgin" to describe this psychological one-in-oneselfness or self-containment. See *Woman's Mysteries* (New York: Harper and Row, 1971), Chapter 11. See also *The Virgin Archetype* by John Layard (Irving, Texas: Spring Publications, Inc., 1974).

3. See *Mandala,* Jose and Miriam Argüelles (Berkeley: Shambala Publications, 1972). Also, *Aion,* C. G. Jung, Volume 9ii of the *Collected Works* (Princeton: Princeton University Press, 1959; first published 1951), paragraphs 352ff.

4. This writer's correlation of the four elements and the four functions springs from her own experience. It would be simplistic to assume such a neat correspondence at all times and for everyone else; the reader is invited to play with these ideas about quaternities and see which—if any—associations are with meaning for her own life. Edward Edinger, in *Ego and Archetype* (New York: G. P. Putnam's Sons, 1972), p. 265, says that the four elements cannot be definitely assigned to any of the four functions. "It seems rather that the structuring pattern of fourness can emerge in a variety of contexts to bring order and differentiation to experience."

Two authors whose experience has led them to the same correspondence as in this book, however, are Ralph Metzner, the consciousness researcher (see *Know Your Type: Maps of Identity,* Garden City: Anchor Books, 1979) and Liz Greene (see *Relating,* New York: Samuel Weiser, Inc. 1978).

The ancient symbols earth, air, water and fire each have several associations apart from the ones suggested in these chapters.

5. See, among many possible references, *Psychology and Religion,* C. G. Jung. Vol. 11 of the *Collected Works* (Princeton: Princeton University Press, 1958), paragraphs 98 and 332, and *Man and His Symbols,* C. G. Jung *et al.* (Garden City: Doubleday and Co., Inc., 1964), especially pp. 200 and 240.

Also the article by Fr. Gerhard Frei in the appendix of Fr. Victor White's *God and the Unconscious* (Chicago: Henry Regnery Co., 1953), pp. 249ff. This is the book that, for many, dots the i's and crosses the t's in the dialogue between religion and analytical or Jungian psychology. Another well-known give and take between these two disciplines is found in the writing of Martin Buber (see *Eclipse of God,* New York: Harper and Row, 1952) and Jung's response (found in *Answer to Buber,* in Volume 18 of the *Collected Works,* Princeton: Princeton University Press, written in 1952).

See also "C. G. Jung and Religion" by Regina Bechtle, S. C. in *Psyche and Spirit,* John Heaney, ed. (New York: Paulist Press, 1966), and "Jungian Psychology and Christian Spirituality," three articles by Robert Doran, S. J. in *Review for Religious,* Vol. 38, numbers 4–6, 1979.

III The View From the Top of the Tower

Air

THERE IS SOMETHING curiously appealing about Barbara's tower and its appearance. Her father does not choose to cast her into a dungeon, nor does he lock her up in a cell. He doesn't confine her to a spare room of their house, but has built this tall cylindrical structure. As though he is the instrument of some higher power, he creates a home for Barbara that reaches upward and suggests aiming high . . . climbing . . . ascending . . .

What would it be like to live encapsulated in such space? We thought of how the roundness or squareness of the tower mirrored Barbara's call to completeness. In tandem with that, she is also immersed in space that almost urges her to rise above the earth level and penetrate the realm of the heavens. Uplifting, we call such environments. We mustn't denigrate the earth qualities with which Barbara's story began—not at all, for she needs them. It's just that she must not stay bound to the earth; there is more for her. She needs to add to her make-up. The shape of the tower, pointing to the higher reaches, urges her to do this.[1]

From the testimony of many of history's prisoners, we might speculate that Barbara will learn to make the most of the few resources she has in the tower. Two of these resources are her small windows. Remember, she is very high and she can see very far. Once Barbara becomes aware of the uppermost area of her tower, she discovers that she has access to broad vistas and horizons. She can see in one direction and to its opposite. And, up in the top of the tower, the air flows in and out from one side to the other.

This new perspective and this free-flowing of the air are like physical preparations of the young woman's spirit for the new vistas and flow of thought which are soon to come her way. Again, there is something about Barbara's physical setting that is a reflection of what is about to happen inwardly. (This business of the places we live in and the places we visit speaking to us of what is happening internally is so commonplace as to be almost beneath our notice.[2] We are more affected by our environments than we realize, however; conscious attention to them will often give us clues—synchronistic clues, we might call them—to the spiritual tasks confronting us at the moment.[3])

Barbara's task at this point in her inner story is to become at ease with the air in her nature, to let that billow up and permeate her. Of the woman for whom air—or thought, idea—flows freely (that is, her thinking function is well-developed) we say there is a lightness, an airiness about her. She can take flight in imagination, spread her wings, learn to fly. She is blessed with the ability to rise above the earth level and, thereby, gain perspective on her own life and the lives of others. Lifted up, she can uplift those around her, refresh them with a certain breeziness.

The air-woman has a freedom about her, like the birds and other creatures of the air. Even if her exterior circumstances are confining (as Barbara's certainly were), her mind can be free and its horizons infinite.

We can, of course, contain too much air. There's the person so in the clouds she just floats away, like a balloon, or the woman who is puffed up, inflated, "puts on airs." Too much air can produce the person who lives only in her upper regions, her head, with little or no connectedness to her earth nature. We see how important it has been for Barbara to have grounded herself in her earth-ness at the start of her story.

Sometimes when we are too airy, we turn into windstorms, into hurricanes and even tornadoes. We become one who whips others up and causes fires to spread. With our words and mental ferment we can turn whatever environment we enter into a whirlwind and keep it stirred up—and earn for ourselves the name of windbag, be called "full of hot air."

Or, the opposite can happen; we may never develop our air-nature, never get off the ground. By paying little or no attention to ideas and new views, we become stale and stagnant. No fresh air moves in us when our air-nature is stifled, nor does any fresh air emanate from us. We can't breathe deeply, and we become suffocating and lifeless both to ourselves and to others. We are like birds with clipped wings that can't fly, or, to use another airless example, we become like bread that won't rise . . . unleavened, flat, heavy.

Air comes into Barbara's life through her two windows, then new thought comes in through them in an even more unusual way. Hidden among the daily necessities of her life (a few slices of bread, some fruit, perhaps a clean dress) is "fresh air" in the form of words about a new religion.

The daily stuff of most women's lives has traditionally and honorably been the basic domestic fare: food, clothing, shelter. Mixed in among these, the word can be found—whether it be the Word of Scripture, as was the case with Barbara, or the message inherent in ordinary things, carriers of sacred mystery in very homely form. We have but to look for it, take time, train ourselves to see. Barbara is able to see and hear the word because her life is one of stillness. She has learned, apparently, to wait for whatever is to be sent her way. She has learned receptivity.

Already, even at this early point in her story, we see how much Barbara has grown beyond the girl child who blandly let herself be sealed off. Developing first her earth-nature and then her air-nature has given her the strength, for the first time, to reach out on her own behalf. Barbara does a very bold thing. She sends out a secret letter by her one thin connection to the world, her basket on the rope. Rather than letting her new-found ideas remain in the sky, she brings them down to earth, maintaining her familiarity with the ground. There is a dialogue between heaven and earth (or upper and lower) in this part of her story that presages well for the future. Barbara has begun to value her life enough to take risks for herself.[4]

We know not how, for the legend is so vague, but a human carrier of the Word is transported into Barbara's life. She, whose story began with an overpowering harmful masculine presence, is sent (almost by *deus ex machina*) helpful masculine power, a priest of the Church. And from him she learns how to make sense of the ideas which have blown through her tower and the new horizons she has sighted.[5]

---

1. There is a wide body of writing on the symbolism of the tower. See, especially, *Psychological Types,* C. G. Jung. Vol. 6 of the *Collected Works* (Princeton: Princeton University Press, 1971; originally published, 1921), paragraphs 390ff. The tower is also a scriptural image, with meaning ranging from presumption (as in the tower of Babel) to stronghold. Mary, like the bride of the Canticles, is called "tower of David" and "tower of ivory," in reference to her strengths. See also Chapter V, note 11.

2. See *Hallowed Be This House,* Thomas Howard (Wheaton, IL: Harold Shaw Publishers, 1979; originally published as *Splendor in the Ordinary*) for thoughts on the layers of meaning in our dwelling places.

3. See *The Tao of Psychology,* Jean Shinoda Bolen (New York: Harper and Row, 1979) for an excellent explanation of Jung's concept of synchronicity.

4. Among the several associations for baskets are those that have to do with birth, as in Moses' story. The basket has the shape of the maternal body. Barbara's story, too, is about birth.

5. One of Barbara's emblems is a peacock feather, with its "eye" at the end. It reminds us of how she came to see more clearly, and of the all-seeing eye of God which watched over the motherless girl. The peacock is also, like the phoenix, a bird of resurrection; supposedly, it grows feathers that are more beautiful each year of its life. Again, Barbara is connected to an image of birth. The peacock's many colors make it, like the rainbow, a symbol of totality. Barbara's other emblems are the palm, for her martyrdom, the sword by which she met her death, torches and cannon, and the chalice and host.

IV The Third Window in the Tower

Water

THE PRIEST, according to our tale, baptizes Barbara. She is washed by water and we are told of the resulting growth in her personality, as Barbara defies her father openly for the first time. In a really daring action, she has a third window added to her tower: an ever-present reminder of the Trinity.

How Barbara has changed! We saw that her assimilation of earth-ness and air-ness (or, to switch back to the psychological language we have chosen to parallel the symbolic, the differentiation of sensation and thinking) led to an increase of personal strength. Now as a third element—water—becomes an integral part of Barbara's story, she grows even stronger and is able to act publicly in her own cause.

Look what she does: Barbara rearranges the stones which have encased her, taking control over the physical matter and space in which she lives, rather than being completely subject to them. The result of her action is a new window on her world, an enlarged perspective. Now she will get more air, more light, a broader view. With the expansion of her personality, she acquires the feminine wisdom to alter the stuff of her environment . . . in the manner of women moving furniture and changing the decoration of their homes (caves, tepees, igloos, castles) throughout history.

The story has it that the third window represents the third person of the Trinity, the Holy Spirit. We also spoke, earlier, of the number four representing wholeness. If this is so, then going from two to three is a sign of growth toward wholeness. The third window provides a bridging outlook between the two views already available to Barbara; it brings things together. Like a third eye, the third window reconciles her previous either/or viewpoint.[1] Barbara, without articulating so much in words, has witnessed in stone to her own evolving. We may be doing the same thing when we "add a window" to our space, letting others see in more clearly and allowing ourselves to see out in a new direction.

Notice too how Barbara's relationship to the masculine has shifted its focus. Now, instead of passively obeying her father, as she did at the beginning of her story when she let herself be led unprotestingly into prison, Barbara finds the courage to speak for herself. In other words, now the masculine power *outside* is not nearly as immediate as her own *inner* strength. She has made a transition necessary for all women who would attend to their souls: the "man within" Barbara has become activated, making the man without less significant.

The teachings of the Church and the waters of baptism have brought about this change in Barbara, we are told, but we must not overlook the human channel by which these were brought—the priest of the story. Imagine the young woman, cut off from all human companionship for we know not how long. Her experience of men has, apparently, been only of her terrible father. Sent, literally, as a gift from God, an entirely different sort of man—a spiritual father—comes into her life, carrying the qualities of wisdom and caring and healing. He, in contrast to her natural father, is a conscious ally. It would have been nearly impossible for her *not* to have cared deeply for him, to have loved him. The apocryphal *Acts of Saint Barbara* tells us that his name was Valentinium, a name we associate with love . . . a graceful accident of history.

For a woman to find the masculine within herself and establish a relationship to it, she dearly needs at least one fine human model of what is manly, in an evolved form. She may not be as fortunate as Barbara, having someone sent into her life. She may have to look to men in public life, or admired on the screen or in sports arenas, or her good male models may come to her from behind classroom lecterns or church pulpits or from the pages of the books to which she responds. She is very lucky if father or brothers or men of her growing-up years have filled this slot.

But she is most truly blessed who is gifted with a close—even covenanted— relationship with a man of real quality ("kything", some call it[2]). Not only can his maleness lead her to the connection with her own so-called masculine qualities, but—even more—the joy of such partners in each other is an external reflection of the potential unions of male and female and human and divine energies *within her* . . . the inner marriages or wedding feasts to which we are each invited.[3] Spoken of in religious language, this parallel is well-described by the author of the latter part of the Book of Isaiah:

The bridegroom shall rejoice over the bride,
and thy God shall rejoice over thee.[4]

The image of a man and a woman who love each other is one of our most beautiful ongoing ways to learn about the inward love relationships of the human soul. We will explore this in more detail in Chapter VI.

Barbara's story, before it ends, indicates that she discovers there is only one love, God's love—and that our human loves are incarnations of it. Perhaps, at the top of her tower, she read Paul's words:

You are always in my heart. . . . I tell the truth when I say that my deep feeling for you comes from the heart of Christ Jesus.[5]

as she found herself unable to separate her human love from the divine, its Source and Prototype.[6]

In ancient days, women of Babylon and Greece would go up to a holy mountain (that is, rise above their everyday worlds) and be made love to by a strange man, one whom they would never see again, so that their ability to experience relatedness in its abstract, person-transcending form would be aroused.[7] The story of Barbara, with the hero dropped into her high tower out of nowhere, has this same quality to it.

So we see that two changes have come about in this section of Barbara's story: her valuing of her faith to the extent that she lets her heart rule her head about how to celebrate it, and her ability to be related to another person. Both are connected with what we call the feeling function, that very subjective aspect of ourselves which helps us evaluate how much things and people and ideas mean to us. It has been called the function of relationship.

Feeling is well-symbolized by the element of water, for—like the springs of living water we speak of—it rises up from the core of us. Water . . . for baptism, only a small amount, but within each of us, oceans. The woman who is at ease with her wateriness is fluid and supple, a channel through which feeling can flow in and out. Those in her company, as a result, find themselves refreshed, their thirst quenched. She is sung about with lines like "You come and pour yourself on me," and her pouring out makes gardens grow, deserts bloom.

If Barbara, if we, did not develop the feeling side of personality, she/we might become dried up and parched. But, too often, we cut ourselves off from our ability to feel because it is so risky, so painful to do so. *Too much* water, we have reasoned at some unconscious level, will drown us—or, at the very least, release floods which may threaten to overwhelm both ourselves and others. We could, we sense, give our water-woman sides too much leeway, let the crack in the dike break and become overflowing, gushing women, the sort who inundate themselves and others with the contents of their depths . . . and force others to put up flood-control barriers against them. We even say, "I never cry, because I'm afraid if I start I won't be able to stop," and speak of seas or rivers of tears and waves of grief. As a result, many a woman cuts herself off from her feeling side, and each year shrivels up a little more, like a grape turning into a raisin, like a leaf in the advancing fall as it loses its sap.

A poignant example of this can be seen among women who live on the streets of big cities. They often look twice their ages, wrinkled and drawn by thirty. Their difficult lives are partially responsible for this, of course, but their lack of feeling—which is very obvious in their manner—may also be an active cause. If your home is the sidewalk of Los Angeles or New York, you can't afford to ponder the value of your life too closely; the fountain of youth literally dries up.[8]

Barbara's father is enraged by his daughter's daring act; she has publicly testified to her ability to love. She has not dried up in her isolated solitude. We can picture him furiously prying open the entrance at the base of the tower, and perhaps we even feel a twinge of recognition: Have we not, as *we* have risked, been broken into by the critical voice inside which finds such fault with who we are and what we are doing? ("You can't do it," it says; "you'll fail." "How dare you even try?" it goes on.)

The angry man races up the stairs inside the tower to grab his captive daughter by her long hair, and hurls Barbara out the window. The legend tells us that her guardian angel catches her and eases her down, not just onto the land but into a ravine in a thick wood. She is not the first to be rescued from a hopeless situation by a guardian angel.

Barbara has gone from the earth at the bottom of the tower, to the air at its top, to the wateriness of baptism and then a forest ravine. Her environment—as before—changes to reflect her inner state; a ravine in the woods was probably as damp and water-logged as Barbara felt herself to be after experiencing the watery depths of her nature.[9] Again, her father is the agent for her necessary next step. He, the person we thought was the villain of the story, is turning out to be the catalyst *without* which Barbara would have stayed a little girl.[10]

She has emerged from her incubation container.[11] And she must have asked, as so many of her sisters emerging from homes and sheltering parents and outgrown jobs and completed relationships throughout history have asked, "Can I make it on my own?"

---

1. See *Psychology and Alchemy,* C. G. Jung, Vol. 12 of the *Collected Works* (Princeton: Princeton University Press, 1953; originally published, 1944), paragraph 31. Another interesting look at the number three by Jung is in his analysis of the fairy tale horse that goes from three-leggedness to four-leggedness in "The Phenomenology of the Spirit in Fairytales" in Volume 9i of the *Collected Works* (Princeton: Princeton University Press, 1959; originally published in 1948), paragraphs 425ff.

2. See Madeleine L'Engle's books, especially *A Wind In the Door* (New York: Dell Publishing Co., 1973), where she uses this word (from the old "kith", as in "kith and kin") to mean bondedness between partners by means of the energy circuit they have established. The kything reaches across miles and all impediments. I am indebted to Louis Savary and Patricia Berne (see their *Prayerways,* New York: Harper and Row, 1980) for this reference. Eleanor Bertine also writes movingly of the same phenomenon, using a different vocabulary, in *Human Relationships* (New York: David McKay Co., Inc., 1958).

3. See "Bewitchment," a study of the hero figure in "The Twelve Dancing Princesses" by Ann and Barry Ulanov, in *Quadrant,* Vol. 11, No. 2, Winter 1978.

4. Isaiah 62:5. See John Sanford's fine book, *The Invisible Partners* (New York: Paulist Press, 1980), pp. 113ff. We should note in passing that there are those who consider the bride and bridegroom image to be a discriminatory one, because the masculine figure is equated with God and the feminine with our humanity. The implication, for some, is that this makes them unequal and is, therefore, sexist (see Rosemary Radford Reuther's work, for example). This argument ignores the fact that, as is often pointed out, there are scriptural examples of the feminine side of God. Can we not see God as androgynous—and ourselves made in that image—rather than delete from our heritage such beautiful images as the one above?

5. Philippians 1:7–8.

6. See "Intimacy," Part IV of *Silent Music,* William Johnston, S. J. (New York: Harper and Row, 1976) on spiritual friendship and alternative relationships. For a cross-cultural overview of the same topic see Part II of *Nature, Man and Woman* by the late Alan Watts (New York: Vintage Books, 1970). His position is close to that of tantra yoga.
   Barbara didn't have the option of an external marriage relationship to reflect the inner unions. A good book (with a Wild West title) on the ideal of the "individuation marriage" is *Marriage: Dead or Alive* by Adolf Guggenbühl-Craig (Irving, Texas: Spring Publications, 1977).

7. See "The Sacred Marriage," Chapter 11 of *Woman's Mysteries* by M. Esther Harding, for a description of the value of Eros in women's lives, ancient and modern. Also see her *The Way of All Women* (New York: Harper and Row, rev. ed. 1970). James Hillman, dealing with the same theme, says: "Reflection may make consciousness, but love makes soul" (*The Myth of Analysis,* New York: Harper and Row, 1976).

8. The literature of analytical psychology, in which this work is rooted, makes a distinction between the feeling function in the personality, and feelings. For the source reference, see *Psychological Types,* C. G. Jung. Vol. 6 of the *Collected Works* (Princeton: Princeton University Press, 1971; originally published, 1921), paragraphs 723ff., or, more simply, *Man and His Symbols,* C. G. Jung (Garden City: Doubleday Co., Inc., 1964), p. 61. Another helpful study is in James Hillman's section of *Jung's Typology* (with M. L. von Franz. Irving, Texas: Spring Publications, Inc., 1979), especially Chapter IV.

9. In a study of the fairy tale "The Handless Maiden," in *Problems of the Feminine in Fairy Tales,* Marie-Louise von Franz speaks of the need for women to accept loneliness consciously; in this story, as in Barbara's, the forest—nature in its simplest state—is the place where the heroine can do this (Irving, Texas: Spring Publications, Inc., 1976), pp. 85ff. This is the loneliness Jesus spoke of when telling us about families being divided (Luke 12:52), and when speaking of the narrow gate through which we must pass, the gate too small to let us pass through with our customary collective group (Matthew 7:13).

10. Remember, according to the legend, that Barbara's father is named Dioscorus. The name comes from Greek lore, meaning "sons of Zeus." That the father bears such a name is an indication of his power, and his importance to his daughter's development.

11. Erich Neumann's work, *The Great Mother,* (Princeton: Princeton University Press, 1953) is relevant in connection with being contained and leaving the container. See especially Chapter 15, "Spiritual Transformation."

In the Tarot deck there is the card of the tower being destroyed. Barbara's tower is not struck by lightning, as is this one, but the meaning is similar. The outgrown/destroyed/vacated tower is, according to Alfred Douglas in *The Tarot* (Baltimore: Penguin Books, 1973), representative of an outdated philosophy that won't meet new conditions. "Life itself is in a state of constant flux, and no merely human construction can hope to survive if it cannot adapt," he writes (p. 101).

V Barbara and Her Story Are Completed

Fire

BARBARA, like Dante in *The Inferno,* comes to her senses in a dark forest. In this place, which is now her home, she will have to use all the inner resources which were being brought to life during her tower days. She needs to put her earth quality to work to find nourishment from the land and to sensitize her to the movements of the animals whose home she now shares. It is earth in us that helps us listen to our bodies and know what they need done for them.

And Barbara's air side, her wits and the learning she has acquired, is what she needs to plan how to protect herself and survive. She is suffering and will suffer more; it is her reason and her understanding of the teachings of her faith which will help her know how to offer this pain, do something with it.

And, surely, her watery, feeling nature will be needed more than ever it was during her days of enclosure. So completely on her own, the only comfort she has will be her feeling that her faith (and the person who embodied this faith for her, wherever he may now be) is worth what she now suffers for it.

We have been talking about psychospiritual development—in Barbara, in ourselves—in terms of the harmony of the four elements of antiquity and what they might correspond to in the personality. The fire-woman in Barbara has not yet had much of a chance to emerge, but now, at the end of her time, this aspect of herself is called into being.[1] Some pictures of Barbara even show her empty tower behind her, shot through with flames.

What is fire in each of us? The mystics of all faiths have used fire-language to describe the spark of God's life at our centers. John of the Cross called it "the living flame," the Quakers have their Inward Light, and spirituals are sung about "this little light of mine." Teilhard is often quoted as saying that when we harness for God the energies of love, it will be the second time in history that fire has been discovered. All echo the words of Jesus about the light within us that should not be hidden.[2]

Barbara is now totally without human support. There are no serving women to supply her simple daily needs of food and clothing, no tower to encase her, no one to talk to or touch or be touched by, not even a despot father to value her in his own inverted way. There are no people to sustain her, only the divine Presence.

If Barbara can experience herself as a container of that spark within—the scriptural language is that we are "temples of the Holy Spirit," the Spirit that came like flames on Pentecost—she will have a reason to survive. (Viktor Frankl's well-known report of the survivors of concentration camps[3] is a present-day example of how such experience saves. Those who lived through the horrors of detention in the camps, Frankl observed, were not necessarily the healthiest and strongest. They were the people with a sense of meaning to their lives; they were about something more than themselves.)

Barbara, to survive her wilderness experience, needs to stay aware of the flame within her. This alone can transform her living and make it worthwhile under such dismal circumstances. Her conviction that she is light-bearer, God-carrier, will give her life purpose. Some postulate that this sort of "spiritual maternity" may come more easily to women because of their capacity for physical maternity (whether or not the latter is ever realized).[4]

We speak of women whose fire-nature is in play as glowing and radiant, words often associated with the bride and the expectant mother. It is at such times that women are very aware of the divine spark within. The Talmudic tradition speaks of this radiance as the *shekinah,* the (feminine) sparks of God that permeate all creation.

The woman who is in touch with this transmuting and enlightening fire in herself is she who has developed her intuition well. Somehow, she "just knows" things; she is able to be and to allow and to let it happen and to surrender to this so-called sixth sense. Women like this warm and shine, effect change more by their presence than by their words or actions.[5] It is the function of intuition that helps us pay attention to the subtle inner flickerings of Spirit.

Yet we fear the fire within. We know it can flare up to raging proportions, burning us up, burning us out. Leonard Cohen's song tells about Joan of Arc's realization of this way of being immolated:

> *. . . then she clearly understood*
> *If He was fire,*
> *Then she must be wood.*[6]

And many a woman consciously or unconsciously dampens this flame rather than have it consume her. She turns herself into a Snow Queen, constructing her own ice palace—and we say she lacks fire or, worse, call her an iceberg or a cold fish.

After some time—who knows how long? as long as is necessary for Barbara to become Barbara-unto-herself—our heroine's father finds her. He drags her before a local judge, the spokesperson for collective authority, and is given official sanction for his cruelty. The voice of the group often goes contrary to our inner directives; Barbara has chosen to save the higher good. She refuses to give up Christianity, even when tortured. Her faith flames up, burns brightly within her. Her light really shines. We have seen Barbara evolve from a girl with no sense of "I" to a young woman with a fine and spirited sense of herself, on to real maturity, where she is able and willing to let something greater than "I" rule her soul.[7]

Barbara's father, unwittingly (as always), takes her to a place—the mountaintop—that is an image of the spiritual height she has achieved. Even to the end of her life, the dialogue between Barbara's outer environment and her inner experience goes on. This man of twisted values drags Barbara up the mountainside by her long hair, symbol of her vulnerability and femininity.[8] Here he, who in such a strange way has been the cause of his daughter's womanly development, cuts off her head with its long tresses.

As Barbara dies, the burning within her flares up even more brightly into an ecstatic, searing vision of her God, in the manner of Teresa of Avila, pierced by fiery arrows, and of Moses and Ezekiel and all those who have found God clothed in flame. Like her earlier sister Psyche, and her later sister Rapunzel, Barbara's story ends in marriage, but it is the heavenly bridegroom who takes her to his kingdom where they live happily ever after. Because Barbara has become completed, the feminine functions of her soul each developed and blended together and her masculinity claimed for herself, she is ready for this external marriage.

Her story is not quite over, however. As an epilogue, a postscript of fire is added: "a tremendous storm with lightning broke out, and Barbara's father was struck and killed by a fiery bolt." It is like a sign from the sky of her final victory, a storm which involves all four elements whirled together (as wind, rain, lightning, mountain peak) announcing the successful coming together of the elements in Barbara. The father is destroyed not by Barbara or by God, but by the forces of nature; he was not in harmony with them.[9]

Saint Barbara's legend, with all its layers of meaning, ends. We have no idea how old Barbara was . . . she had as many years as were needed for her to approach her completion, just as we each have. We need not worry that we are starting too late on this life-task, saying ". . . my life is half over and, look, I'm just now learning about these essential things." God's time, as has so often been noted, is not our time; there is a time for us to have been busy about the things of the world—and there is a time for us to discover the person inside waiting to be born. We have the rest of our lives for this second adventure, although (at first) attention to our own lives seems strange after decades of endless giving. A very common expression among church and temple women in fact, is "I feel guilty taking time for myself. . . ."

Our focus on others and our busyness can, however, be an avoidance of the need to refill inner wells that are long overdrawn. And if we are called to more self-knowledge, and then turn our backs on the call, we can expect the powerful contents of the world within to unleash themselves in *some* way. They may find space in our lives through inexplicable speech and behavior, or they may show up in psychosomatic symptoms, to name just two possibilities. And the result? our spiritual lives are affected, negatively, by that which is unknown and unrelated to in us. Jesus, using the same image of wholeness we have found in this story, speaks to us of the personal cost if we "decide to build a tower" and then do not continue with the work.[10]

Barbara's story began as she was enclosed in external space that looked like wholeness—her tower. This physical space set the stage for the end of her story: the development of psychological and spiritual wholeness. Sometimes in medieval art, Barbara is shown holding her tower; she has her arms around the concept of totality, can grasp it, manage it.[11] It is only when she is able to do this that we call her *Saint* Barbara, for "wholeness" and "holiness" are similar words.

She has pictured for us, her latter-day sisters, what *we* might become: women with our earthy, airy, watery and fiery gifts of God functioning in feminine ways, women in relationship to the maleness within us, women ruled by the God living in our depths. Barbara's story can, it seems, be your story and mine.

1. Barbara's development, as we have imagined it, has gone from her earth-nature, through her air- and water-natures, to, finally, her fire-nature. For each of us, there might be a different sequence. See *Psychological Types* and the many Jung-oriented writers on the dominant function, the auxiliary functions and the inferior function. The inferior function—that which is least natural to us—is thought of as the link to the depths of the unconscious, and is therefore called "the function of religious experience." Indeed, one can only partially realize it and must, in fact, eventually bow to it if it is to be integrated with the other three.

Dr. von Franz (in *Jung's Typology,* p. 19) compares the inferior function to a horse that can never be ruled, but on which one can at least learn to stay seated . . . most of the time.

2. See Jung's lengthy description of the Scintilla, or spark, in *Mysterium Coniunctionis,* Vol. 14 of the *Collected Works* (Princeton: Princeton University Press, 1970; originally published 1954), paragraph 42ff.

3. Viktor Frankl, *Man's Search for Meaning* (New York: Washington Square Press, 1965).

4. On this "Is anatomy destiny?" issue, see "Womanhood and the Inner Space," Chapter 7 of *Identity: Youth and Crisis* by Erik Erikson (New York: W. W. Norton and Co., 1968). He says yes, anatomy is psychological destiny, to a certain extent. And Simone de Beauvoir, in *The Second Sex* (New York: Bantam Books, 1978; originally published 1953), indicates that women, because birth-givers, tend toward seeing God as immanent rather than transcendent—but, unfortunately, her implication is that this is an *inferior* (rather than a complementary) tendency.

5. See Chapter IX, "The Rainmaker Ideal," in *Knowing Woman,* Irene Claremont de Castillejo (New York: Harper and Row, 1973), for a classic description of this sort of person.

6. "Joan of Arc," Leonard Cohen, © Stranger Music, B. M. I.

7. For a complete description of these stages of development, see *The Origins and History of Consciousness,* Erich Neumann (Princeton: Princeton University Press, 1954), especially the section on "Centroversion and the Stages of Life." See also a somewhat more readable treatment, *The Way of Individuation* by Jolande Jacobi (London: Hodder and Stoughton, 1967; U.S. edition, Harcourt Brace and World, Inc., New York).

8. Long hair, as a symbol, has different associations. Because it comes from the head and is a part of the body that "reaches out," it is connected with thought and intellectual curiosity—and also spiritual development, because it is "up," higher, closer to heaven (for early peoples who saw the sky as the home of the divine). Christian tradition pictures the gentle action of the woman who wiped Jesus' feet with her hair, associating long hair with womankind. Giving up of tresses for centuries was connected with women who were either renouncing their sexuality, by entering the cloister, or those who had betrayed it, such as witches (their heads were shaved before trial). And for both sexes, long hair equaled vulnerability: an enemy could capture you by the hair (or beard), just as Barbara's father did.

9. The Mahayana Buddhists say the lightning bolt stands for the overpowering light of truth in which all falsehood is destroyed.

10. Luke 14:28–30.

11. We have seen how the tower, like so many of the transforming symbols, can carry a double meaning. It is a pointer to wholeness and put-togetherness, self-containment. Paradoxically, it is also the barrier that must be transcended if that same wholeness is to be achieved. Scripture and ancient lore are full of such two-faced symbols (for instance, the serpent); they tell us that the very thing that seems to be the biggest stumbling block to our development is often the way to it. The ultimate example of such a double-sided symbol, of course, is the cross, image of totality and the joy of resurrection—but we must embrace its pain before we know its glory.

VI A Little Background

WOMEN TODAY, unlike the women of Barbara's time, are offered a bewildering smorgasbord of approaches to their development. And women with allegiance to organized religions often find their churches and synagogues and temples battlegrounds for border skirmishes that reflect, in microcosm, the uproars over women's growth issues in general. The fallout affects the important matter of their spiritual growth, the focus of this small book and a topic that is—admittedly—a keg of worms.

Approaches to the Spirituality of Women

Three of the approaches to feminine spirituality from which we have to choose are:

• the "total woman" approach, based on a word-for-word reading of women's role in Scripture. The advantage of this view is that it stresses the uniqueness of both men and women, rather than opting for a unisex sort of world. Therein lies its truth. The enormous drawback of this approach, of course, is that it limits women and their growth (inner and outer) to traditional roles, and suggests that they find meaning for their life through relationship to Mr. Right. Some of the extremes of the charismatic renewal which have overstressed obedience and "headship" reflect this mindset. It can be very seductive—especially because, in contrast to militant feminism, it helps keep the peace in families and in institutions. We might ask, however, at what price to the women involved is that peace bought?[1]

• the views represented by feminist theologians, a polarization of opposition to the "total woman" stance. Some women in this category primarily petition for equal representation in their churches and temples, as they are now structured; others seek reform of patriarchal systems that have devalued women's contributions for centuries. These outspoken critics of sexism in religious institutions have waged battle against exclusive language in liturgical celebrations (". . . all men," for example, to mean "all people") and have raised consciousness throughout the ranks about the feminine qualities of God. They have campaigned—successfully—to open doors to ministry by women, doors which were tightly sealed until recently. As models, they have the great women saints of their tradition; Catholic feminists, for instance, draw inspiration from women like Catherine of Siena and Teresa of Avila.

The heartbreaking drawback to the story of *some* of the women in this group is that their struggle for equality begins and ends in rage, and in separation from the people and institutions they most hope to influence. Just as we inquired of the women who subscribe to a fundamentalist stance, "What does this do to them?", we may also question the inner or spiritual effects on a woman of a position that is, basically, a reaction *against* rather than an embracing *of* something.[2] At least one feminist writer says that our new sacred texts must be the women's literature of our time, rather than the Scriptures of our traditions; the ultimate reaction to the too-slow-to-move institution is indifference.[3]

• a third way, a celebration of the complementariness of the masculine and the feminine, both in each person and all of creation. This approach, which can be called an androgynous view (from the ancient idea of the androgyne, the person embodying the characteristics of both sexes), somehow seems an alternative between the two extremes discussed above. It has won favor with some religious feminists, those who stress the need for reform of the institutions so that mutuality of men and women is possible and women's unique gifts are honored to the extent men's gifts have always been. It is also becoming a touchstone for former "total women" (in the popular sense of that phrase), who knew in their hearts that the differences between the sexes need to be not only respected, but also celebrated.

The main point about androgynous spirituality, however, is that the equality between masculine and feminine of which it speaks is primarily in reference to our inner worlds, not the outer world of the roles we fill. Androgyny is a very old concept, going back to the hermaphroditic legends of the ancients, and finding a zenith time in pre-Confucian China. Its most articulate spokesperson in modern times has been Carl Gustav Jung, whose analytical psychology tells us an enormous amount about the feminine and masculine energies in each of us, men and women alike. A large part of Dr. Jung's work is concerned with the balance or harmony of these complements within us, and how the reconciliation of these opposites leads to increasing wholeness/holiness,[4] or another sort of "total woman"—one like Barbara. (Sometimes the word androgyny is misunderstood to mean the same thing as "unisex"—no differentiation between the genders. This is really a misreading of it, as a study of its derivation will show; it refers to complementarity between the genders, not a blending of them into oneness.)

Thus, according to this line of thought, whether a woman is a homemaker, confined to bed and board by her husband (and the Altar and Rosary Society by her parish), or whether she is celebrating Mass or driving a Mack truck is not the *primary* point. The *most* important consideration is whether or not she experiences herself as a container in which both feminine and masculine forces are present, in dialogue, working together, headed for union with the God dwelling in her soul— for when this happens, she is maturing spiritually, and that is what we are here to do. The fascinating "next step" is that inner wholeness seems to attract, in magnet fashion, outer situations that reflect it. Thus we find women who are carriers of both the feminine and the masculine energies in harmony having doors "miraculously" opened for them in the outer world, doors that give them opportunities for the sort of equality other women have gone to the barricades for—and failed to achieve.

One of the beauties of Jung's thought is that it reminds us of how the external world mirrors our internal world, a concept congruent with today's incarnational theology and the outer-sign-reflecting-inner-truth themes that run through all the world's Scriptures. A recurring thread in Dr. Jung's eighteen volumes of collected works and in his autobiography is that we find harmony in our outer life to the extent that we have sought it in the inner. (This is not to discount the very necessary attention to external signs and needs. The language we hear, the roles we see people filling and the omissions we so easily overlook all must, of course, be attended to. Nothing written here is an argument for privatized spirituality in a world so filled with injustices as ours. The point is that the inner life is the starting point for the outer.)

Saint Barbara's story, as we have embroidered it, shows us in relief the ingredients of this inner world: the feminine energy, the masculine energy, and the God-life in the soul. The first two, in appropriate relation to each other, give us the total—or androgynous—Barbara; the third, the divine energy of which we are all vessels, is what makes her a saint. Let's explore these three ingredients or energies of the soul and their relationships to each other to see whether or not they speak to us of a feminine spirituality which is nourishing and complete.[5]

The Feminine Principle

The natural place for the so-called "feminine" energy in a woman is at the layer with which she meets the outer world, the level of her ego or sense of who she is. In Barbara's story we saw four components of her personality—thinking, feeling, sensation and intuition—and spoke about her development of each of these in a womanly way. If we had been looking at a man's story, we would have spoken about developing these four functions in manly ways.

But what do these words "feminine" and "masculine" or "womanly" and "manly" mean? We've heard them so much, used them so broadly and unspecifically, become so aware that one person's "masculine" or "feminine" is very different from another's, that (like the word "love") they have become fuzzy. Going back to early thought about the androgyne helps us here, for we find that both "masculine" and "feminine" are used as ways of describing types of activity. The association comes from the differences between men and women physically, but also goes far beyond that. Even the most primitive peoples could see, for instance, that men's larger size and generally greater physical strength made them the ones to go out hunting tigers and to protect the caves. The mode of behavior, then, that was about assertion, penetration, action, doing, and dynamism—even when directed toward the inner world—became associated with maleness. Women, being child-bearers, were forced by nature to learn to wait, to practice stillness, to just be. The sort of activity in both inner and outer life that was about such things became known as activity which was feminine. The male and female roles in sexual union pointed up these two modalities, and all of nature echoed the eternal flow between these complementary poles of giving and receiving.[6]

None of this is to say, as many authors have pointed out, that women don't also need to be doers, nor men not need to be be-ers; in fact, the whole point of the androgynous person is that he or she is both, that he or she has both types of energy flowing and available as needed. The spiritual distinction between the sexes comes about, according to this school of thought, in at just what level of the person each of these two forces operates. In women, it is natural to face the world psychologically with the feminine energy, to have an ego colored by what the Chinese call the *yin* energy—just as women face the world physically in their unique way. In men, the opposite or *yang* energy is most naturally externalized. Ego-formation is usually considered the first task of the spiritual growth process along the lines we've been discussing.

In Barbara's story, we correlated the four ego functions which can be developed (and shot through with the *yin*-type energy) with the four elements of antiquity. We have spoken of a woman's earth-nature, her air-nature, her water-nature, and her fire-nature. As mentioned earlier, there is no universal agreement as to the correspondence of the elements to the four psychological functions,[7] but more than one source agrees with the schema used here:

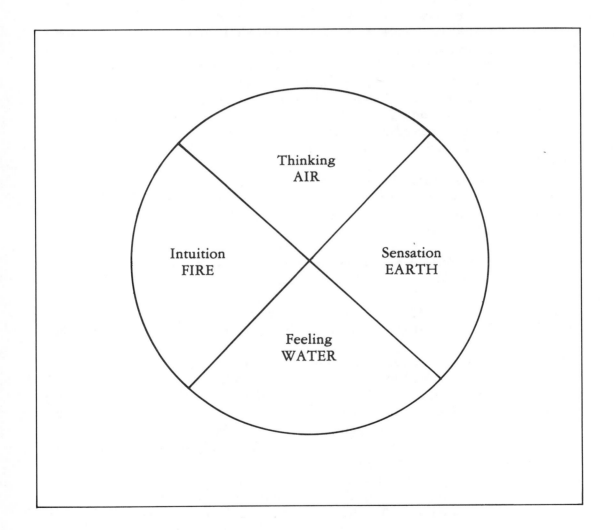

The reader can try on the above correlations for size, use them as they are, find those more suitable for herself, or decide against any such congruencies. (The appendix of this book contains exercises that will help the reader explore both the totality of the feminine and each of the elements in her life. These have been worked out by some of the women mentioned in the Introduction and this writer over a period of several years and found useful.)

It has been helpful to several of us concerned with the ideas in this book to think in terms of "too much earth, air, water, fire" or "too little . . ." or "just enough . . ." as well as to work with the more technical language. The "too much" or "too little" come up in psychological translation as the shadow or not-yet-known sides of our natures which need to be recognized and accepted. These are the very areas in which there is the most hope for development.[8]

The four quadrants pictured above form a circle, the image of wholeness . . . but they also form a cross, the sign of suffering. The inner work we are speaking of can, indeed, be experienced at times as crucifixion. Heading toward wholeness is not easy, but then separation from part of ourselves and the God within us is even more difficult.

Toni Wolff, an associate of Dr. Jung's, is known for her description of the four women in every woman—that is, the four functions as they appear when charged with the feminine energy.[9] She suggests that within each woman are the following constellations of energy:

- the THINKING WOMAN, such as the good teacher or the goddess Minerva
- the FEELING WOMAN or companion, a *femme inspiratrice* such as St. Clare was to St. Francis
- the SENSATION WOMAN, typified by the earth mother or the artist
- the INTUITION WOMAN, a sort of mediatrix, as were the prophetesses of old

The ideal or goal of this part of the inner work (or the "opus" as it is sometimes called) would be to have all four of these women in one's self evolved to *some* degree, and available to be called upon when needed. We spoke of Barbara getting all four of the functions together; she was "finished" by the end of her story. The legend is, however, just that—a legend, a fairy tale, and it pictures for us an ideal situation. Our own stories aren't likely to have such a neatly wrapped-up ending as Barbara's, but we can be in process toward the ideal: having the two ways of perceiving (sensation and intuition) and the two ways of judging (thinking and feeling) available to us to *some* degree. Toni Wolff makes the point that it is the inner woman associated with the inferior function (see Chapter V, note 1) that "cannot, as a rule, be lived concretely . . . because she is so different from whichever inner woman comes most naturally. She must therefore be expressed on the symbolic level."[10]

If only one or two of the women listed above develops in the personality, as happens if we do not give high priority to our inner lives, she or they may take it over. And if that woman within grows in a negative direction, we can end up taken over by, say, the Terrible Mother or Supermom (too much earth) or by the intuitive gone awry, the Witch (too much fire).

Often our dreams will show us where the overabundances or lacks of inner feminine life are. One woman using the correlation between the functions and the elements in this book dreamed of a woman gasping for air as she kept getting pulled down into the earth. She felt this to be a true picture of the imbalance among the women within herself, for she had devoted her entire life to nurturing others in true Earth Mother fashion and had not given her thinking side much attention. Fortunately, she understood the meaning of the dream, and she understood that she could use her earth mother's great nurturing power to care for the neglected air woman. And this is what she did, taking more and more time during the week to read, ponder and discuss what she was learning. Some months later, she had another dream about these two inner women. In it, she was a sort of scientific gardener, plotting in great detail a beautiful garden (attention to the earth, which she certainly didn't want to forget), making charts of where the beds would be and studying the best way to grow each plant (the thinking woman in action). She felt the dream to be about how she had honored these two inner women in herself, and she also spoke of how the garden would need both water and fire (the sun) in order for it to grow. The garden was an image of her own blooming, just as it is in Saint Barbara's story.

The Virgin Mary is, of course, a time-honored model of the woman with all four of the inner women's qualities highly developed. And sometimes the Virgin, or a queen, or a great goddess, or a fairy godmother, or other timeless women of extraordinary luminosity even appear in our dreams, as if to hold out to us a vision of what we might become.[11]

Our task is to develop a sense of ourself meeting the world—and, also, turning toward the inner world, for the ego does both of these things—in a way characterized by the feminine. Numerous writers have testified as to how difficult it is for modern women to do this, largely because we have so few models of women who joyfully incarnate the feminine energy.[12] The feminine is characterized, as was mentioned earlier, by receptivity—the ability to listen and to wait, by a static rather than dynamic stance—but it is the stasis of expectancy, not mere passivity. The feminine energy flows from the outside inward; it is centripetal or waning, yielding. And as such, it is also associated with synthesis and fusion and unifying, for that is what happens when things are taken in. And when things are taken in, they are in relationship; they look at each other and connect rather than separate. It is the feminine energy in women and in men which brings things together. The feminine is also about valuing that which is beautiful (as at the end of the Psyche myth). And it is about reconciling through love that which is irreconcilable through logic.[13]

The life of Mary, the mother of Jesus, echoes all these qualities of the feminine. Devotion to her by Christians through the centuries has been one of the few ways Western men and women have kept the feminine alive in their own lives and their institutions, for Mary is very much about listening and waiting and expecting. She is about saying "yes" and about yielding. She is about love and relationship, just as was Jesus—a man with his feminine side highly developed.

Both the men we live and work with, and the churches and other religious institutions we care about, are sorely in need of the feminine principle in their lives; it is the neglected side of the *yin-yang* pairing in the Western world. If women do not consciously carry the feminine, modeling it, meeting the world with it and making it present for others, who will? Surely we cannot expect men to do this— although many are trying well to be aware of this need in their lives and in the world. A feminine spirituality that starts with the ego formed in this way gives a woman an equality that no amount of external activism can hope to produce, and also makes it possible for her to have the masculine energy in her nature on the "inside" where it rightly belongs. Let's move on now to consider the development of the masculine (or *yang*) energy in women, a task which usually cannot be handled too well until she has a strong feminine ego-orientation. There is a never-ending uncovering process of both types of energy in us—and each, as it develops, increasingly throws the other into relief, helping it become more and more clearly defined.

The Masculine Principle

Just as the feminine in women can be characterized by inner women, the masculine can be described as an inner man (or men). And, according to the thought of Jung and his followers, "his" function is twofold: to back up the external feminine ego and to link it to the depths of her soul, the God-life within. Obviously, we are moving here from the realm of psychology to that of religion. The psychology needs attending to, however, for if the feminine energies in the woman aren't in place and working for her, then the more assertive masculine energies may take their place. When that happens, she weakens or loses the bridge to the divine life dwelling within her. When the maleness and the femaleness in her being are each doing their own job, however, she is "on her thread"; then we can speak of feminine spirituality.

(Of course, we want to note that God's grace can overcome any amount of imbalance in one's personality. The lives of the saints give us ample evidence of persons who, by our lights, weren't too tightly wired up—and yet, because of their fidelity to the life of the Creator in their souls, shone like the bright stars Paul wrote of to the Philippians.)

We saw how Barbara began by handing over her inner and her outer life to the men around her—first her father, then the bearer of the Word: a harmful and then a helpful masculine figure. She later became able to take back that masculine or action-oriented energy and use it for herself. Once she had it within her for her own use, she was able to find the strength to make a public statement on her own behalf (the third window), to survive in the wilderness, to face death bravely and, finally, to unite with her God.

What are the qualities of the energy we are calling "masculine"? We spoke of it being that flow in both women and men that reaches out, takes action, risks, gets things done. For these reasons, it is associated with focused thought and speech; the mouth is sometimes spoken of as masculine, while the listening ear is feminine.

The *yang* energy, to go back to the Chinese terms, flows from the person; that is, it is centrifugal or waxing, and may be concerned both with inner and outer reality (that is, introverted or extraverted). The taking-in energy in the person, the feminine energy, merges and meshes things (both inwardly and outwardly) into new totalities; the going-out force, in which the contents of the darkness are brought into light, tends to show things in their separate parts. The *yang* energy is about discrimination, analysis, what we often refer to as "left-brain" activity. Reaching out is akin to reaching up, and the masculine energy in both men and women is usually credited with the thrust toward the spirit realm, the vision of that which is beyond (while it is the feminine, according to this line of thought, which brings that spiritual experience and the theory behind it down to earth for practical use). The masculine energy stresses individuality, separateness, while the feminine is about relationship. The masculine enables us to be alone.

A woman who has committed herself to the spiritual life, or even just to successful day-to-day living, knows how much she needs these *yang* qualities. She welcomes increasing awareness of the inner masculine, which often shows up in her dreams as men who help or hinder her, or are just on the sidelines, waiting to be allowed some space in her life.

A woman teacher and healer, for instance, tells of her pleasure at meeting one aspect of the masculine within her in the dream presence of a scholarly fellow named Bernie Shapiro. Bernie is very bright, almost a walking encyclopedia! Whenever she wants lots of factual information at her fingertips, or wants to teach something clearly and succinctly, she calls on Bernie to help her. Were he not harnessed by his possessor, he could very well manifest himself in her life as an opinionated show-off, dropping names and information wildly. Because she knows him, however, and has established a relationship with him, he works for her. He has been brought to consciousness, not left to operate in the dark.

We not only meet inner figures in dream form, but we also meet them in real life. Whenever our path crosses that of someone who strongly attracts or repels us, we can hypothesize that he or she carries some quality within us which we haven't yet realized. The experience of falling in love is the most powerful example of this phenomenon, called projection in the language of psychology. The attractions—and repulsions—give us amazingly clear pictures of as-yet-unknown parts of ourselves, parts that are asking to become conscious and integrated with the rest of our being.

Another woman met an aspect of the masculine in herself in projected form when she found herself unexpectedly hooked on the TV rock group Sha Na Na. Here she was, a professional woman in her forties whose usual TV fare was *Masterpiece Theatre* and *Sixty Minutes,* rushing home nightly to catch reruns of ten greased-down musicians with black leather jackets, tight pants and boots, gold chains and bare chests! When she realized how strong was her connection to these talented but very different (for her) men, she saw that they represented a side of the masculine energy in her that hadn't yet been recognized, much less put to use. Now, the inner man or men, just like the inner women we spoke of earlier, may be typical of any of the four functions—and here in tenfold strength were men who were *definitely* about sensation! Everything, from their constant hair-combing, to their Elvis-like gyrations, to their double-meaning jokes about their girlfriends (just barely passing the TV censor) told her that she had some masculine energy still in darkness within her that had to do with the senses and sexuality.

The very fact that she needed *ten* of these men to give her the message told her how unconscious this part of herself was! (Apparently, her earlier encounters with *one* such man—like some of Marlon Brando's earlier characters, or John Travolta in *Saturday Night Fever*—hadn't been enough to stir the slumbering sensation man within into consciousness.) The appearance of inner figures in groups also indicates that the energy they stand for is still in very primitive, archaic form. It hasn't become individualized, which is what will happen as it gets closer to consciousness. And the youth of the men in Sha Na Na (most of whom look like boys just out of high school, though their professionalism belies that) told her that this part of herself was still immature, very much in need of growing up—as well as a source of young, new energy.[14]

How did she establish a relationship to this part of the masculine in herself? She put together (as she drove to work) a composite of the Sha Na Na singers, designing one fantasy figure who was a product of her own creativity, named him, and took him out for "airings;" as she called them. She bought a bike and went out on it, accompanied by her imaginary friend (who would probably have preferred a motorcycle). She took pains to build even more physical activity into her life, calling on his strength and appreciation of the body to support her. When last heard from she was considering buying a copy of *The Joy of Sex.*

Does all this sound a little . . . well, crazy? It isn't something she spends a lot of time with, nor does she confuse fantasy with reality; this is just a tool to help her get to know an unknown part of herself. Interestingly, as the sensation man in her soul became more conscious, her fascination with the TV performers dwindled. She had learned from and withdrawn her projection on them. The whole point is that, left in darkness, this sort of energy with all its power can sabotage a woman; birthed and appreciated and assigned its proper place in her life, it/he is a great help to her as she strives to be well-rounded.

What's more, learning to take back energy that is properly one's own from men we only see at a distance trains us to do the same when we project the inner man—positive or not-so-positive—on a man we really know. (Our clue that this has happened is a strong feeling, pro or con, about the person.) We can then do the necessary reclaiming for ourselves of what we have given away, even when we fall in love—*especially* when we fall in love! This reclaiming can then open the door for relationship founded on reality, rather than one based on our god-like expectations of a very human man, expectations no mortal could possibly live up to.

There may be one well-developed inner man in a woman's life who is a composite of thinker, feeler, intuiter and senser, a male counterpart to the Mary or queen type of woman figure we spoke of earlier. He stands for the totality of that which is masculine, showing us what the inner man can become. Jesus often takes this role, even for non-Christian women. There are pictures from late medieval times showing Jesus standing on an orb or sphere—the round symbol of totality—and symbols of fire, air, water and earth in each of the four corners of the drawing. The pictures seem to say that Jesus is the sum of all the ingredients that comprise wholeness.[15] Meditating on the Lord and his different strengths is one way today's women can get to know the man within them better—or you might also want to put it the other way around, saying that knowing the man within is one of the ways to Jesus.

The Christian reader may ask, "Why bother with anyone *but* Jesus? Why spend time with greased-up TV singers or the walking encyclopedia man?" For some people, such attention to the imperfect parts of themselves is too human; they just want to stay with the divine. To skip over the clues to consciousness that are sent to us, however, is to deny the unfolding process that our particular inner life has chosen. There is a tendency in us toward completeness, toward becoming

from *Psychology and Alchemy* by C. G. Jung
original from *Le Propriétaire des choses,* Glanville (Fr.), 1482 now in the private collection of the C. G. Jung Institute, Zurich

perfected—and if our dreams and waking life send us inner figures that fall short of the ideal, they are telling us that these are the areas to which we need to pay attention. Further, if God is the Giver of the clues to our unfolding (whether these clues be dream images or people sent into our lives), then we can trust that we are being sent exactly what we most need at any time.

Spiritual transformation or the individuation process (simply, becoming the individual we were born to become) comes about as the conscious part of one's being dialogues with the contents of the unconscious, which reveal themselves through the sorts of hints (dreams, projections, fantasies, simple daily events, etc.) we've been exploring here. If we pay attention to these indicators—sometimes sublime, sometimes ridiculous or even dreadful—we learn about the next step we are being called to take.

The literature of analytical psychology describes over and over the ways in which women who do not know the masculine energy in themselves give it away to the men (or masculine institutions, like the churches) in their lives. We drape them with it or project it onto them in both its positive and its negative forms, and place upon the men so chosen the impossible burden of being our other halves. We expect the men we love (or hate) to complete us, not knowing that this is the task of our own inner masculinity. We then evaluate ourselves through the eyes of these men (or institutions) and their opinions of us, staying dependent little girls. The "total woman" spirituality seems based, in large part, on this sort of giving away of one's inner resources.

Sometimes, when women see that this is what they have been doing, they set out to reclaim the masculine energy of their souls for themselves, as the woman hooked on Sha Na Na did. They reel it back in, so to speak, but—sometimes—instead of the masculine becoming a complement to the feminine, it takes over the ego-space *vacated by* the weak or absent feminine energy. Then we see women who end up meeting the world in mannish ways, even looking mannish—but never as successfully as men, because this masculine energy in a woman is that which is "other," not that which is hers most naturally. It is in the wrong place, doing a task for which it is not intended. The woman is as if bewitched by the reverse side of her personality (sometimes, misleadingly, called the "inferior side").

Spirituality that is characterized by a lot of teeth-gritting hard work and worrying ("if you're not suffering, you can't be growing"), and lots of super-serious intellectual abstraction and talking (the mouth, remember, being associated with the outpouring of ideas from the man within), seems to appeal to women who carry "him" outwardly. This sort of spirituality seems like having the words without the music; it lacks heart and relatedness; it's cold. The woman's *primary* focus may become external matters rather than the internal love relationship with God. She may find herself trying too hard to make things happen, shelving the listening and surrendering to and trusting in whatever is sent her way that is such a necessary balance to action. Again, this is not to deny the external concerns that need attention; it's just a matter of priorities, of seeking first the kingdom of God and truly believing that all else will surely be added if this seeking is placed first.

So, we have described two ways in which the masculine energies in a woman can be out of place: giving them away to real men, or letting them elbow out the feminine. And we have a wonderful example of a female creature who oscillates between super-girlishness (her masculinity projected onto a real man—or frog) and externalized mannishness (her masculine energies possessing her ego) in America's own sweetheart, Miss Piggy! We could say that Piggy just hasn't got her masculinity working for her. Sometimes it gets deposited on Kermit the Frog and she, all aflutter, sees herself only in fantasy relationship to him as carrier of her other half. She feigns helplessness, bats her baby blues, talks of "little old moi." At other times, Piggy reclaims the maleness she's given away. It takes her over. She becomes a wild boar, blasting anyone in her path with "Watch it, Buster!" and neat karate chops, as she pilots the *Swine Trek* through the universe or barrels a four-rigger down Interstate 91 (Piggy's CB handle is Ham Hock).

Now, if she could just develop a conscious relationship to the man *within* her— but then she wouldn't be Miss Piggy. And we wouldn't have such a lovable picture of the contradictory ways *we* extravert our inner masculinity. No wonder she's so popular!

For women, the man within is designed to make their receptivity active (and for men, the reverse is true: the *woman* within makes their activity receptive). It is an essential step then, in feminine spirituality according to the androgynous model being discussed in this chapter, that a woman have her inner man in his place. That place is as a back-up to her feminine ego and as mediator to her depths. If we compare "his" role psychospiritually to our physical experience, we could think of the inner man as a counterpart to the skeleton that holds the outer portions of the body firmly, connecting them to the vital centers of the person. If the inner man is *not* in place, he will be somewhere else, out of place—animus problems, these are called, the animus being Jung's term for the masculine in a woman. And these problems cause pain and havoc, wrecked relationships and unnecessary confrontation between men and women, rather than bonding and partnership.[16] But if he can be brought to light, embraced and redeemed—and stories like *Beauty and the Beast* and the legend of Psyche tell us about this—then he will be that sure connection to the divine Life within. We might even ask, as John did in his First Letter, "If you do not love your brother, how can you love God?"[17]

The God Dwelling Within

We have been speaking about three energies in the person: the feminine and the masculine and the divine, or that which is Other, transpersonal. Below is a super-simple diagram of the appropriate places for each of these three inner energies in women. Well, yes, it really *is* presumptuous to draw little pictures of the soul! (Do some readers remember parochial school versions of the soul from the 1930's and 1940's: a glass of water or milk with little black specks in it? Not only was this soul-model bad theology, but racist as well.) The reader is asked to forgive the unsophistication inherent in rendering the soul in a drawing; it's to help us visualize more clearly what this chapter is all about.

(a) the level of the ego, which includes consciousness and the personal unconscious or shadow, and also the persona or covering we adopt to meet the world. Normally, this outer layer is the home of the energy associated with one's biological gender. For women, then, it would be at this soul-space that the four inner women (sensation, intuition, thinking and feeling) live; it is the realm of the feminine.

(b) a deeper, unconscious level. This is the suitable residence of the contrasexual energy; in a woman, therefore, it is the home of the masculine. And "his" task, as we have been observing, is to mediate the Life at the center to the ego, *and* to support the feminine ego with strength and the other qualities associated with "*yang*" energy.

(c) God's Life in the soul. Now, of course, we can't and won't limit the Almighty to a spot on a chart; the God Life not only floods the entire soul, but all of creation, so that it is as if we move in a "sea of God." God is not only immanent, but also transcendent.

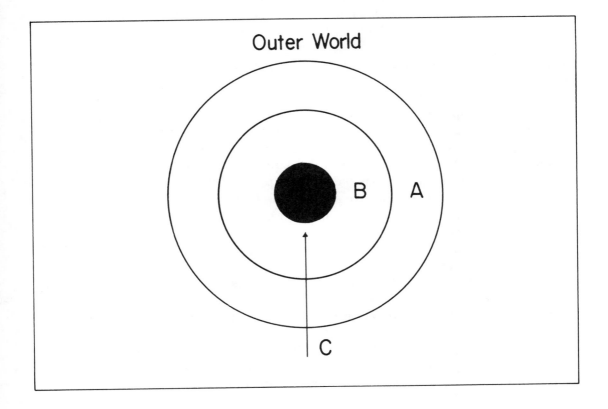

On the other hand, those familiar with centering prayer or those who have found mandalas helpful for meditation will perhaps agree that there is something appropriate about God being at the center, at the deepest level of the soul. It gives us a sense of this divine Life being the focal point of our being. Women's dreams often represent this greater-than-themselves force by the super-women we spoke of earlier: the Virgin, the queen and so forth.[18]

With a model like this one, then, spiritual growth can be described as a twofold process:

• the person becomes increasingly conscious about the activity of both the feminine and the masculine in herself. As she becomes more and more aware of both, and their relationship to each other, the feminine nature with which she contains the divine Life becomes a more finely tuned instrument. And the masculine channel to that Life grows stronger, surer.

For some women, this balance of masculine and feminine in their natural places just happens—it is a gift, one which usually comes from parents who model externally the sort of relationship a young girl needs to develop interiorly. Many other women, however, will testify to the ways in which they feel blocked from meeting the world with their natural feminine qualities, and the struggle they feel between the forces within. "Things just aren't in sync," they may say.

• at the same time, the person becomes increasingly aware of the God Life for which she is a temple or vessel, through attention to it in all the ways of asceticism we know so well: prayer, sacramental life, immersion in Scripture, spiritual reading and study, periodic examens, journal keeping, spiritual direction, meditation, community life and so forth. Of course, this Life within us can transform our souls with or without our help, and can even flame up and illuminate one whose surrounding "layers" of the soul are a mess. The kingdom of heaven is not only likened to a treasure to be uncovered, but to a merchant who goes out and does what must be done to obtain the pearl of great price. The tendency toward union comes both from our finite level, as we dig deeper, and from God's dimension.[19] If grace builds upon nature, however, our attention to all the forces within us is just good stewardship of our lives; we do not need a present-day Quietism that leaves all the effort to God.

The goal of spiritual growth, according to this model (and some others, as well), is that the person's operating center shift from the ego-level to the God-realm, the kingdom within if you like. Barbara was "able to let something greater than 'I' rule her soul," our story told us. All the "I live, now not I but Christ lives in me . . ."[20] expressions in the world's Scriptures are about this reorganization of the personality, which is come to by a never-ending process of deaths to old ways of being and rebirths into new ways (which in turn will become old ways in need of transformation). This is how the paschal mystery is lived out in our lives.

The ego needs to remain strong; it is how we face both the inner and outer worlds. But it surrenders its primacy in the person's life, becoming more and more like a clear lens. External events are taken in through this "lens" and communicated to the God who lives within one—and internal light from that divine Indwelling is reflected through the ego-lens out to the world. The person, literally, lets her light shine and sparkles like the stars.[21]

Compartmentalized charts like the one above don't do justice to the beautiful mystery of this growth process; they are sometimes scorned as reductionist, "Mickey Mouse" approaches. Let's return then to the way that the Christian tradition, among others, has taught us about this holy happening. Rather than analyzing it clinically, Scripture gives us the wonderful image of what it means when both feminine and masculine come together and also when God and the person are joined: the marriage, the wedding feast. A picture of a bride and groom is about a love relationship, and that is the right tone when we experience the "bride" and "bridegroom" who reside in us as inner woman, inner man—and who must love each other if they are to function as partners. It is even more true as an image when we speak of the mystical marriage between the soul and its Creator; the saints have reported for us the ecstatic heights of love to which their union with God has brought them.

No wonder we spend so much time wrapped up in our fascination with *outer* male/female comings together, sometimes in the form of being in love with love ourselves, other times in our flocking to sex-saturated movies and TV shows. We seem to have "an endless, aching need" (as the song *The Rose* tells us) for being one half of a pair or, at the very least, watching that happen in the lives of others. Think, for example, of how the royal wedding of Britain's Prince Charles and Lady Diana kept people around the world glued to their television sets at early morning hours. Our longing to be part of such external joinings is very much about our longing for both the inner joinings. It is the need for the union of the pairs of opposites within us that is constantly being constellated and stirred up, asking to be minded.

In the best of all possible worlds, we would each have the blessing of being sent a close, supporting love relationship that would reflect and teach us about the interior relationships; ". . . Where one may barely pass, two may go easily . . ." says Charles Williams, the English novelist.[22] An outer pairing, as we mentioned in connection with Barbara and her priest friend, can be a wonderful aid to the inner conjunctions in a world that doesn't exactly support our attempts to grow spiritually. It can be a beautiful sign of what can potentially happen within us—the coming together of masculine and feminine, the coming together of God and the soul—but it *can't take the place of* the inner marriages. And when we ask an outer relationship to carry the weight of *all* our longing for togetherness, we place far too heavy a burden on it.[23] The two inner marriages—the lesser one reflecting the greater, sacred one—are what each of us is called to. We may or may not also have the gift of the third, or external, joining, but the first two are possible for everyone.

So, like any good love story—like Saint Barbara's story—the androgynous view of feminine spirituality we've been exploring ends in marriage. It is a joyous image. The spiritual life is serious, yes, and often painful and wracking, but it is also filled with the best happiness earth has to offer, with song, with dance, with ecstasy. We tend to make our inner explorations so heavy and ponderous, settling for much less than the marriage delights. It's almost as though we can't believe that such joy is possible. It is, for each of us.[24]

The reader will recognize that the spiritual evolving described above is, truly, a life's work. And it is sacred work. In our time, Morton Kelsey and John Sanford, their names often paired, have given believers a body of writing that clarifies and unites both the religious and the psychological views on this subject. Their premise, as followers of Jung's thought, is that the tendency—indeed, the longing—for wholeness is also the religious instinct.[25] The works of these two men are much recommended for those who would explore this meshing of analytical psychology and religion more thoroughly, for what has been presented here is just the simplest door-opener (or glimpse into the tower, to get back to our Barbara-based images). The other references throughout the notes in this book add up to a bibliography on the feminine, mostly from the same viewpoint. It is hoped that the interested reader will find in them the nuances this more introductory book has, of necessity, bypassed, and she will be *most* fortunate if she is able to find another to act as a guide or companion for the journey of which they speak.

The subject of feminine spirituality is, as we mentioned earlier, a controversial one. So, in the close of the twentieth century, is the broader topic of spiritual growth in general. The 1960's were, for many members of religious institutions, times of involvement in social concerns, as the serving and giving aspects of belief were emphasized. The 1970's saw a pendulum-swing in the opposite direction, as the inner life again became emphasized and prayer groups flourished. There also tended to be a polarization of trends in spirituality between the subjective, incarnational viewpoint (represented, for example, in Roman Catholic circles by such authors as Adrian van Kaam, John Powell, Eugene Kennedy and Henri Nouwen) and a more classical, objective viewpoint focusing on the indwelling of God and the forgetting of one's self.

Now, in the 1980's, we see reaction set in again, with the 1970's labeled "The Me Decade" and a time of "New Narcissism." Among Christians, this is often characterized by put-downs of "Jesus-and-me spirituality." Such criticisms are not without cause; they express impatience with endless introspection in a world desperately in need of social action.

This book, obviously, is concerned with the inner life more than its outward overflow—not because the latter is not highly valued, but because this writer's experience is rooted in the tradition that says collective, social, institutional change starts with individuals who change. This idea has been popularly expressed through the centuries as "you can't give what you don't have," a belief that the quality of what we do to help others and our world depends upon the quality of who we are. The Chinese, whose roots are androgynous, speak of being "on the flow." They have many stories about the person whose inner balance of energies reflects in holographic form the whole flow of creation, and who makes things happen just by his or her presence. Our Western tales of men like Francis of Assisi, in whose company even a fierce wolf turned lamb-like, are that sort of testimony to the priority of the inner life for the person who would be an agent of external change.[26]

But we don't have to make an artificial choice between being Martha or Mary, between the active or the contemplative life. The ideal for most of us is a life incorporating both—not "either/or" but "both/and." Thomas Aquinas said it well: we are here "to contemplate and give to others the fruits of contemplation," which is really just a paraphrase of "love others as you love yourself."

Saint Barbara did just that. Her story, as we have walked through it with her, is very inner, very personal, but she has lived and been appealed to and helped in we know not how many ways for almost two thousand years. In the Middle Ages, in fact, she was one of the Fourteen Holy Helpers invoked for protection against the worst of disasters. The Eastern churches still call her Saint and Great Martyr Barbara.[27]

Each of us, like Barbara, has the call to God-saturated wholeness, the completeness of the tower. Many—even most—may never hear the call, and many who hear may choose to ignore it. But on behalf of those who do respond with joy to the invitation, men and women alike, let's close with the appeal:

Saint Barbara, pray for us!

1. See Stephen B. Clark. *Man and Woman in Christ* (Ann Arbor: Servant Publishing Co., 1980.) and *The Total Woman* by Marabel Morgan (New York: Pocket Books, 1973).

2. See for example, Mary Daly's *Beyond God the Father* (Boston: Beacon Press, 1973), p. 43, and the proposals to trade patriarchy in western religion for matriarchy and the goddess (see *The Politics of Women's Spirituality,* Charlene Spretnak, ed., Garden City: Doubleday and Co., Inc., 1981).

3. Carol P. Christ, *Diving Deep and Surfacing: Women Writers on the Spiritual Quest* (Boston: Beacon Press, 1980).

4. As hinted at the end of Barbara's story, these two words are often used synonymously, as though psychological wholeness was the equivalent of holiness. A study of their derivation shows that though they are close, they are not the same. Believers will want to be sure they remember that holiness includes the action of God's grace, rather than ending up with a neo-Pelagian stance that says "If I just get myself together, I'll be there." The best reference on androgyny is *Androgyny* by June Singer (Garden City: Anchor Books, 1977).

5. What follows is just the briefest sketch of enormously complex ideas, reduced to give the beginning reader an overview. And—an important point—it is written from the standpoint of the heterosexual personality. For a succinct summary of the differences for the homosexual person, see *Caring* by Morton Kelsey (New York: Paulist Press, 1981), Chapter 7, note 4.

6. One source of further elaboration on these two energies of all creation is John Sanford's *The Invisible Partners,* pp. 7ff.

7. See note 4, Chapter II. James Hillman (*op. cit.,* p. 76) is one who prefers not to make any such correspondences.

8. See John Sanford's *Evil: The Shadow Side of Reality* (New York: Crossroad Publishing Co., 1981).

9. Toni Wolff, *Structural Forms of the Feminine Psyche* (privately printed for the C. G. Jung Institute, Zurich, 1956). Hard to come by, but the ideas in this pamphlet may be found in Ulanov, *op. cit.,* Chapter 10, and *The Invisible Partners,* pp. 102ff. See also *The Moon and the Virgin: Reflections on the Archetypal Feminine* by Nor Hall (New York: Harper and Row, 1980).

10. Wolff, *op. cit.,* p. 12.

11. See the remarks about medieval representations of the Queen of Heaven as the fruition of the four elements united in *Mysterium Coniunctionis,* par. 450ff.

12. A superb book is *The Owl Was a Baker's Daughter* by Marion Woodman (Toronto: Inner City Books, 1980). Subtitled "Obesity, Anorexia Nervosa, and the Repressed Feminine" it speaks to women without weight problems as well. It is about the price the body pays for being cut off from the feminine energies.

People of many traditions, including that of analytical psychology, have spoken of the body as a metaphor for the soul. "As a woman is in her body, so she will be in her soul; as she is in her soul, so she will be in the world," paraphrases a quote from author Sam Keen. Virginia Woolf's expression was: "There is a truth to the body."

In *The Tao of the Body* (Los Angeles: Analytical Psychology Club, 1958), Mary Whitehouse describes two extremes: being cut off from the inner world and being overwhelmed by it—and the way the human body reflects those extremes. She says that in the former instance the person's body is rigid and inflexible, repressing; in the latter, the bodily motions are "too much"—hands flying, lots of movement that doesn't seem connected to what the person is saying or doing.

13. See *The Feminine: Spacious as the Sky* by Miriam and Jose Argüelles (Boulder, CO: Shambhala Publications, Inc., 1977), for more images and descriptions of the feminine. A transcultural collection.

14. Sha Na Na is made up of ten singers and instrumentalists who perform rock 'n' roll oldies and earlier sentimental ballads. They do it half straight, half tongue-in-cheek; their motto is "Grease for Peace."

15. See Chapter One of John Sanford's *The Kingdom Within* (New York: J. B. Lippincott Co., 1970) for a fine description of Jesus as exemplar of all four functions at their best. In the same chapter, mention is also made of how Jesus combined both feminine and masculine qualities in his person. There is a tradition from medieval times of the androgyny of Jesus, in the sense that we are using that word in this work. See, for instance, *Psychology and Alchemy* by C. G. Jung, paragraphs 22 and 547.

16. Two books with much more detail on the animus working for and against a woman are *The Invisible Partners* and June Singer's *Boundaries of the Soul* (Garden City: Anchor Books, 1973). See also *Man and His Symbols,* pp. 189ff.

17. 1 John 3:17.

18. See Jung on God-like or "mana" images, the *imago Dei,* e.g., *Psychology and Alchemy* in Volume 12 of the *Collected Works* (Princeton: Princeton University Press, 1953), paragraph 11.

19. See the interesting comparison of the two parables of the treasure and the pearl in *Creation Continues* by Fritz Kunkel (Waco, TX: Word Books, 1973; originally published, 1946), pp. 160ff. Also, *The Kingdom Within,* pp. 39ff. and *Digging Deep,* a good book by Robert L. Schwenck on dream symbolism, a Christian viewpoint (Pecos, NM: Dove Publications, 1979), p. 148.

20. Galatians 2:20.

21. See Daniel 12:3. The literature refers to this connection between the ego and the deep core of one's being as the "ego-Self axis," Self being a non-religious term for that which is greater than our limited (small s) selves. See, for example, Edinger, *op. cit.,* p. 5.

22. Charles Williams, *The Greater Trumps* (Grand Rapids: Wm. B. Eerdmans Publishing Co., 1976; originally published 1932). Romantic love has not enjoyed a good press in recent years, lovers being advised that it will inevitably fade, or—more clinically—that "it is all projection." Research into the emotion of love, however, seems to be one of the psychological trends of the 1980's, and in *The Passionate God* (New York: Paulist Press, 1981) Rosemary Haughton celebrates the unique way in which romantic love allows the divine pattern of ecstatic coming together to break through into our lives.

23. See the treatment of the themes of the inner wedding and external manifestations of it in *The Kingdom Within,* pp. 195–96 and 210ff.

Also, an interesting analysis of our rushes into external relationships that can never take the place of the internal is in *Love and Addiction* by Stanton Peele (New York: Signet Books, 1975).

24. A nice grace note: Saint Barbara, on whose story we've hung our reflections about the inner weddings, is associated with external marriages in Austria. On December 4, her feast day, unmarried members of a household go into the orchards and cut twigs from the cherry trees. These are put in water and set in a dark corner. Those persons whose twigs bloom on Christmas Day are expected to be married within the year.

25. See Ulanov, *op. cit.,* p. 12, for elaboration on the religious instinct.

26. It is a Teilhardian theme that what one does for one's own soul benefits, at the same time, the *anima mundi* or "world soul;" there is a divine ecology. See for example, *The Divine Milieu* (New York: Harper and Row, 1960), pp. 69ff.

27. The Fourteen Holy Helpers, whose feast is celebrated on August 8, were especially popular in Germany at a time when the Black Death ravaged Europe. They were invoked against physical ailments and also diabolical infestation (St. Margaret the Martyr) and terrors of the night (St. Giles of Provence). Devotion to a few of them remains: St. George, St. Christopher, St. Blaise. St. Barbara was invoked for protection against lightning and electrical storms and against an unprovided death, both problems associated with her father. Because of the latter, she is often pictured holding a chalice and host, or a monstrance. She is also patroness of artillery men, stone masons, armorers, carpenters, tilers, prisoners, architects and fortifications (because of her tower life), and of firemen and fireworks makers (because of the lightning bolt at the end of her story), as well as miners, grave diggers, smelters and brewers (an association with her living off the land in her last days?), and hatters and brush makers (because of a Latin pun on her name, which is about beardedness)—and, not to be overlooked, mathematicians (for no discernible reason, other than that in order to be a saint, she had to figure things out)!

Saint Barbara in Song and Verse

Excerpt from *The Ballad of St. Barbara,*
by G. K. Chesterton (1922)

Barbara the beautiful
Had praise of lute and pen:
Her hair was like a summer night
Dark and desired of men.

Her feet like birds from far away
That linger and light in doubt;
And her face was like a window
Where a man's first love looked out.

Her sire was master of many slaves
A hard man of his hands;
They built a tower about her
In the desolate golden lands,

Sealed as the tyrants sealed their tombs,
Planned with an ancient plan,
And set two windows in the tower,
Like the two eyes of a man.

Her father had sailed across the sea
From the harbour of Africa
When all the slaves took up their tools
For the bidding of Barbara.

She smote the bare wall with her hand
And bade them smite again;
She poured them wealth of wine and meat
To stay them in their pain.

And cried through the lifted thunder
Of thronging hammer and hod
'Throw open the third window
In the third name of God.'

Then the hearts failed and the tools fell,
And far toward the foam,
Men saw a shadow on the sands
And her father coming home.

'There were two windows in your tower,
Barbara, Barbara;
For all between the sun and moon
In the lands of Africa.

Hath a man three eyes, Barbara,
A bird three wings,
That you have riven roof and wall
To look upon vain things?'

Her voice was like a wandering thing
That falters yet is free,
Whose soul has drunk in a distant land
Of the rivers of liberty.

'There are more wings than the wind knows
Or eyes than see the sun
In the light of the lost window
And the wind of the doors undone.

For out of the first lattice
Are the red lands that break
And out of the second lattice
Sea like a green snake,

But out of the third lattice
Under low eaves like wings
Is a new corner of the sky
And the other side of things.'

Then he drew sword and drave her
Where the judges sat and said
'Caesar sits above the gods,
Barbara the maid.

Caesar hath made a treaty
With the moon and with the sun,
All the gods that men can praise
Praise him every one.

There is peace with the anointed
Of the scarlet oils of Bel,
With the Fish God, where the whirlpool
Is a winding stair to hell,

With the pathless pyramids of slime,
Where the mitred negro lifts
To his black cherub in the cloud
Abominable gifts,

With the leprous silver cities
Where the dumb priests dance and nod,
But not with the three windows
And the last name of God.'

Barbara the beautiful
Stood up as queen set free,
Whose mouth is set to a terrible cup
And the trumpet of liberty.

'I have looked forth from a window
That no man now shall bar,
Caesar's toppling battle-towers
Shall never stretch so far.

The slaves are dancing in their chains,
The child laughs at the rod,
Because of the bird of the three wings,
And the third face of God.'

Caesar smiled above the gods,
His lip of stone was curled,
His iron armies wound like chains
Round and round the world,

And the strong slayer of his own
That cut down flesh for grass,
Smiled too, and went to his own tower
Like a walking tower of brass,

And the songs ceased and the slaves were dumb;
And far towards the foam
Men saw a shadow on the sands;
And her father coming home. . . .

Blood of his blood upon the sword
Stood red but never dry.
He wiped it slowly, till the blade
Was blue as the blue sky.

But the blue sky split with a thunder-crack,
Spat down a blinding brand,
And all of him lay back and flat
As his shadow on the sand.

This ballad is part of a longer poem by the same name. Saint Barbara is known as the patron saint of artillery men, or "St. Barbara of the Gunners," as Chesterton has it. In the full poem, men at war in France are under fire and one, a Breton, recites the tale above for his comrades. The situation they are in is contrasted with episodes from Barbara's life and the soldiers pray to her as "a stay in sudden death." The poem ends with these verses, which are about the soldier-narrator:

> But he that told the tale went home to his house beside the sea.
> And burned before St. Barbara, the light of the windows three,
> Three candles for an unknown thing, never to come again,
> That opened like the eye of God on Paris in the plain.

A Custom for Saint Barbara's Day from Syria

On December 3, the eve of Saint Barbara's feast day, Christian Syrian families gather for a treat of boiled wheat sweetened with cinnamon, sugar and herbs and decorated with raisins, nuts and pomegranate. Asking Barbara to bless their eyes, the mother of the family takes *khol,* used by the ancient Egyptians as a cosmetic, and places some on the eyelids of all gathered. This song is sung in Arabic:

> Chosen by God, Saint Barbara,
> While your father, the atheist, worshiped stones.
> The rope he brought to hang you
> Was turned into a belt.
> The fire he brought to burn you
> Was turned into clay.
> We prepared cooked wheat.
> Why didn't you come to eat?
> Oh! Saint Barbara, chosen by God.

Barbara's association with eyes no doubt springs from the "eyes" of her tower, the three windows which enabled her to see afar. Another version of this song reads:

> Saint Barbara is running away
> With the neighborhood girls.
> I recognized her from her hands
> And the twinkling in her eyes
> And the bracelet on her wrist.
> Saint Barbara is running away!

(With thanks to Maxine Stephen of Altadena, California)

Barbara's Song

1. My to- wer home did wrap me round,
2. Now be- cause of you, my heart can sing.

My___ heart as cold as it's stone__.

Love of my life, you touch me so___,

The ech- oes spoke:"I am__ a- lone___,"

you fill me up__, I o__- ver- flow__.

No hope in this__, this emp__- ty sound__.

Be- cause of you __ my heart has wings__.

melody: traditional anglo-american ballad

61

Appendix

Some Experiments for the Reader

Symbols from Barbara's Life—and Ours

The following pages are filled with questions, with words and phrases, and with exercises and meditations and prayers based on the symbols in Saint Barbara's story. These are also the symbols of our stories, if we let them be. The reader is invited to browse through these pages, letting a word reach out and speak to her, or an image draw her into itself, working through the exercises at her own pace. The symbols have their own transforming power (see the thoughts on this at the end of the book). Our task is to give some space to a few of them—not necessarily all of them, but the ones that are very personally appealing. We can do this by

- using them in prayer
- using them in meditation
- drawing them or finding pictures of them
- living with them
- carrying them with us in our hearts
- keeping our antennae (you know, those little things on the top of our heads) out for the way a symbol can intrude into our life (externally, when we find ourselves tripping over it; internally, in our dreams and reveries)

- seeding our dreams with them; that is, using a pertinent symbol as part of our night prayer and asking that we be sent dream lights about its meaning in our life
- recalling the associations of the symbol to our own life (what has it meant to us?)
- researching the history of special images, building on the little bit of background given here

We always need to remember that the spiritual growth these symbols point to is the work of the Spirit; we can't force it. We can, however, be facilitators of our own evolution, participating in it consciously and intentionally, rather than just sitting back and hoping it will happen. Patience, gentleness, reverence at the great mystery of God's work in us—these are the qualities called for as we engage in soul-making.

The Four Elements

THE ANCIENT ELEMENTS of earth, air, water and fire are among the most pervasive symbols in the history of the world. We meet them in Greek thought, that of Empedocles and then of Aristotle. To the Greeks they were the substance of which all creation was composed. In the Western world, there is little mention of the four elements during the early Christian days and the Dark Ages, although they flourished as carriers of meaning in the East. However, as Saints Albert and Thomas Aquinas looked backward to classical science in the Middle Ages, they revived interest in the elements. The medieval alchemists used the four elements as symbols in their work, which C. G. Jung has since shown to be an attempt to enact in matter the psychospiritual growth process we have discussed in this book.

As sophistication in the sciences progressed, it became clear that earth, air, water and fire were not the building blocks of the human body. Medical autopsies confirmed this, and in 1661 *The Sceptical Chymist* by Robert Boyle was published, questioning Aristotelian science and its simple four-part description of matter. Still the *images* of the elements remained. They stayed around in astrology, for instance, often in a debased way. Even today, this foursome speaks powerfully to people. In

Los Angeles in 1980, for instance, a beautiful exhibit to honor the bicentennial of the city of Our Lady, Queen of the Angels opened. As viewers walked into a dimly lit, gauze-draped space, music of the spheres blanketed them and they gazed on twenty-eight-foot-high angels of earth, air, water and fire. There were also altars to each of the elements, topped with antique madonnas. No explanation of *why* these basic symbols were used was given—nor was one necessary. The thousands of visitors were being spoken to at a very primary level of their beings. They knew it and responded with awe.[1]

Here are two exercises about all four of the elements in our own life. These are followed by thoughts and questions on each of the elements separately, and then by some suggestions for designing a special day for each of the elements. This is one way to let what they are about sink down into us. A final section has ideas for allowing these four symbols to come together into a whole greater than the sum of all its parts.

Saint Barbara's Story/My Story

As you read the story of Saint Barbara, did you find yourself in any part of it? Are you

- encased in earth?
- letting in air?
- washed with water?
- container of fire?

In general, which of the elements would you say was your most natural one? (We even speak of "being in our element.") Which seem less natural to you and in what order?

My Name

Without doing a lot of thinking about it in advance, write your name in an earthy way, an airy way, a watery way, and a fiery way. The form of your name can vary (Sarah James, Mrs. Jesse James, Sally . . .), even childhood nicknames being used. If you have different things to write with (pen, crayon, pencil) choose the one that fits best for each name; different colors to choose from add to your range of possibilities.

When finished, compare your four names. Did you use the same version for each? Which one came out most like your usual signature? If married, did you use your unmarried name at all? Do any of the names look childlike in style? What differences do you note in color, size of writing, slants, and other qualities? From this exercise, what reactions do you have about your relationship with each of the four elements?

Earth

". . . the earth is filled with the knowledge of the Lord"
—Isaiah 11:9

Earth is the only one of the four elements that can be held in one's hand. It is the only one that can be molded into a form which will remain stable. Earth is the most opaque of the elements, the only one that can't be seen through. The land—or earth—is often spoken of as the mother giving birth to her people: almost all early religions had an earth goddess, and even today people speak of their motherland. Born from earth, we return to her at death. It is appropriate that earth should stand for that which is material and solid in our being, our physical bodies and our senses.

Here are some questions to help us explore our experience of earth and to get a better feeling for its symbolism. The reader can check off those responses that speak strongly to her, and fill in other reactions.

- What are some of the different forms earth can take?

soil	rock	sand	mud
clay	dust	minerals	

- What are your usual contacts with earth?

gardening	caring for house plants
shopping for harvest of the earth	car stuck in the mud
mowing the lawn	kneeling to pray
walking, running	

- What are some other ways people come in contact with earth (even unusual ways)?

construction work	archaeology
being buried	digging to China
earthquakes	backpacking

- What are the properties of earth?

stability, solidity	endurance, lastingness
covering, layered	absorbent, retentive
nourishing, bears food	gives boundaries, limits

- When do you feel or act in earth ways that are helpful?

  nurturing: preparing a meal, caring for others or self, being a rock for others

  bearing fruit: in work, in relationships

  down-to-earthness, not afraid to be earthy

  patience, having the ability to wait

  in touch with my roots, firmly planted, on dry land, on solid ground, getting to the core, practical, feet on the ground

- What is it like to have an overabundance of earth?

heavy	plodding	burying, smothering
materialistic	weighted down	head in the sand
earthbound	carrying a heavy load	stuck in a rut
holed up,		like a clod
in hibernation		feet of clay
dug in		

- What is it like to have too little earth?

  uprooted, ungrounded

  undernourished

  lack of reality, out of this world

  not on firm ground, unstable

  barren, fruitless

  shallow, superficial

  house built on sand

- How does earth handle problems?

absorbs them physically	stands firm
covers them up	outlasts them

- If "earthyness" is that part of you that's about using the senses and being in touch with the physical and material, what are some things you can do to pay attention to and nourish this part of yourself?

  use whatever strengthens the body

  avoid whatever weakens the body

learn to listen to my body

evaluate my material needs and consumption–and my use of possessions–carefully

spend time on the land, with growing things

be with those whose senses are alive, earth-people

A Grounding or Earth Meditation

Find a place indoors or out where you can lie down comfortably, and won't be disturbed. Be sure you are dressed warmly enough, or covered, for the body can become chilled in deep relaxation such as this, called—with good reason—the "pose of a corpse" or *savasana* in hatha yoga. This is also a useful meditative technique for falling asleep.

If there is any way you can actually do this in contact with the earth, all the better.

Step 1. Lie down on your back, and settle yourself comfortably. Let yourself sink into the bed or floor or ground on which you are lying. Adjust each part of your body until it is in its most comfortable position. Notice any areas of tension and relax them. Pay attention to your breathing, and slow it down gradually.

Step 2. Working your way up the body from feet to head, tense each part of it, hold the tensed-up muscles, then release them. Let the just-released part of the body sink down even more deeply.

Feel the points at which the body touches whatever you are lying on; let these become even heavier, as though gravity were drawing all of you downward from these points of contact.

Visualize the floor (or ground) beneath you; next the upper, then the lower layers of the earth, with the pull of gravity coming from the earth's very center, drawing you downward.

Step 3. Now working your way up the body again, can you let your attention focus on each part of it separately, in an appreciative, affirming way? Linger a little longer on any portions that need healing, or which you have neglected in the past, or which have seemed unattractive to you.

Step 4. This meditation is so relaxing you may doze off. Whenever you are ready, however, come back to your normal state by stretching all over a little, then a great deal. If you did snooze before getting all the way up the body, finish up now the as-yet-unappreciated parts.

You may want to end with whatever sort of prayer seems appropriate as a thanksgiving for the way you have been wonderfully formed. You might also want to thank your body for being such a fine home—or temple—for your spirit all these years.

The benefits of this meditation:
- It is a way of, literally, getting grounded and reconnected to our most present material reality—our own flesh and blood and bones, which we all too often skip over.
- It is a prayer of self-blessing and of healing.
- It gives deep relaxation and rest to all the body, including the internal organs.

A Reflection on Being an Earth-Woman

I leaned against a tree and felt a kinship. Now I feel the tree within me . . . a reaching down with my roots, deeper and deeper to the darkness, the Source of life, and reaching out, branching to nourish, to protect, to shade, to grow.

Sometimes what seems like a mighty tree can be eaten inside by a thousand little things and topple during a storm.

I must derive my sustenance from the main Tree and from whatever branch I spring from (my ancestors, my roots, my faith). Earth is when I am *here* to my children, to others . . . stable, unchanging in many ways: my inmost beliefs, my love for them, my caring.

How long do I care for these—how long do I mother?

Earth Mother, it's time now to turn to another self that's been waiting, impatiently, lest she die from neglect.

I am a tree.

Air

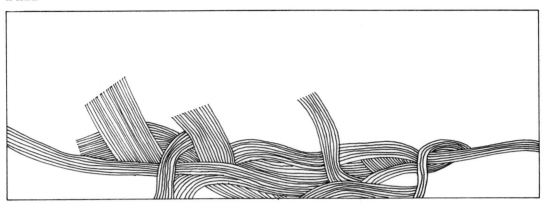

" . . . we who live will meet the Lord in the air"
—I Thessalonians 4:17

Of the four elements air is the only invisible one. All, in some form, are necessary to life, but none more so than air, without which we cannot exist even a moment; it is that creative force that God breathed into the first human. Since ancient times, air has been associated with the part of the human body that, like air, was upward—that is, the head. This connected air to the activities of the mind: thought, reasoning, perception, understanding. When Pope John XXIII spoke of "opening the windows of the Church," he was speaking of letting air—new ideas—in.

The following questions and responses, to which the reader can add, will help to explore the experience of air in our lives.

- What are some of the different forms air can take?

wind	hurricane	tornado
breeze	breathing	sneezing
stale air		

- What are your usual contacts with air?

breathing	sleeping with window open
smelling	hanging out laundry
polluted air	

- What are some other ways people come in contact with air (even unusual ways)?

flying	wind chimes
lung and respiratory ailments	space travel

blowing bubbles   hang gliding
riding magic carpets   birdwatching

- What are the properties of air?

moving   lifts up, rises   volatile
invisible   light in weight   unifying

- When do you feel or act in ways that are helpful?
  breezing along, floating on air, effervescent, on cloud nine
  rising above it all, detached, having an overview, a bird's-eye view,
      having perspective
  aethereal, like a breath of fresh air
  free as a bird, dancing, when I spread my wings and fly,
      flying high, when my heart has wings
  airing my views

- What is it like to have too much air?

puffed up, inflated   full of hot air, a windbag
whirlwind, headstrong   putting on airs
flighty, spacey, high   scattered
living in my head,
    head-tripping,
    beating the air,
    head in the clouds,
    going whichever way the wind blows

- What is it like to have too little air?

stagnant, stuffy   stifled, suffocated
not breathing: dead,   empty-headed
    lifeless
on thin air

- How does air handle problems?
  float above them, rise above them
  blow them away
  analyze them, keep them in the head, talk them to death

- If "airyness" is that part of you that's about using thinking and your mind, what
  are some things you can do to pay attention to and nourish this part of yourself?
  think, read, listen, study
  seek out idea-carriers: people, books, films, programs, etc.
  organize my library
  go where the air is clean and clear
  do breathing exercises
  be with air-people, those whose minds are alive

A Breathing or Air Meditation

This is the simplest sort of prayer or meditation possible—and one of the oldest. It is a way to stay aware of the key idea behind all praying: that God is present. This truth is so basic, so primary that we often skip over it into more complicated praying. This prayer can be done anywhere and at any time: while driving, shopping, listening to sermons, doing housework or officework or schoolwork, at Little League games, while falling asleep or waking up, when ill.

Step 1. Find what seems to be your center spot (for many, it is in or near the heart space).

Step 2. Then, pay attention to your breathing. Imagine, with each incoming breath of air, that you are drawing in God's presence which surrounds you. And with each exhalation, picture that presence going to your centermost place, so that you become filled with it.

Step 3. If you slip away from remembering to do this, just pick it up again easily, with no strain.

Some variations:

- There are people who find it helpful to visualize their center space in some way, as a heart, or a diamond, or a (well) spring, or a light (see the fire meditation). Some just color it—that is, they visualize the color the body itself suggests.
- We are constantly surrounded with people and things that carry God's presence. As you breathe, notice these carriers of the holy, and draw on them for nourishment. Some of these containers of the sacred are:

other people	music	growing things
pictures	symbols	food
scents	books	sun, moon, stars
special places, indoors and outside		

Step 4. A logical result of this practice of the presence of God is that, as we become more aware of the divine presence at our center, we begin to move and speak and act from that place, letting the God within use us as a channel. Christ "dwells by faith in our hearts" (Eph. 3:17; the St. Louis Jesuit's song *Dwelling Place* can be a good trigger for this meditation). Can this awareness become more and more habitual as you mature in this way of prayer?

The benefits of this meditation:

• It is a way to pray always. Since it is tied to our breathing, which continues until the end of our lives, it is a prayer skill we can practice at any time or place all our lives.

A Reflection on Being an Air-Woman

I've always loved the wind, watching trees bow and dance in the breeze, the sound of wild winds tearing around, sleeping outdoors with a cold wind on my face.

After a time of still and sultry air the cleansing wind is most welcome. After a bout of emotion, logical thought helps—the cool breeze of knowing.

How do I experience the wind within me and be air-woman? I can be like a bird, soaring between heaven and earth. My brain gets clearer. I soar in prayer but have to come back to earth. I feel free when I am up there, but there are dangers in trying to fly too high.

I am a bird.

Water

" . . . let her who thirsts come . . . and receive the water of life freely."
—Revelation 22:17

In nearly all legends of creation, water is spoken of as the source of life; think of Genesis, of God hovering over the water. No element is mentioned more often in Scripture than water: water for cleansing, water for baptism, water for punishment, water for refreshment and life, water for transition from one stage of life to the next, water for blessing. It is the most mobile of all the elements, never resting as fire and air may and as earth almost always does. This makes water an image of *change* and of that part of us which we cannot turn off or quell. It is also the element which reflects back.

Here are some watery questions and responses in which to slosh around.

- What are some of the different forms water can take?

ocean, sea	river, stream	pool, lake
spring	rain	tap water
body fluids	liquids we drink	

- What are your usual contacts with water?

showering, bathing, swimming	washing dishes
reconstituting juices, coffee	cooking
drinking	

- What are some other ways people come in contact with water (even unusual ways)?

scuba diving	changing diapers	floods

baptism	fishing	taking a cruise
drowning	boating	

- What are the properties of water?

wetness	mobility, fluidity, adaptability
depth, sinks down	yielding, shapelessness, encompassing
reflection	buoying, suspending
unpredictability	cleansing, dissolving, evaporation

- When do you feel or act in water ways that are helpful?
  pouring myself out, flowing, healing others
  being used as a channel, a canal
  in touch with my depths, still waters run deep
  refreshing, like a cool drink of water, a thirst-quencher
  things inside bubble up, bubble over
  able to bend
  dissolving barriers
  seeking my own level

- What is it like to have an overabundance of water?
  stormy seas, waves of grief, floods of tears
  in over my head, swept away, submerged,
      drowning, in deep water
  misty-eyed, weepy, awash, adrift
  soggy, water-logged, clammy, a wet blanket, saturated,
      all wet, a drip, liquidated
  gushing, babbling
  melting, knees turning to water, passion rising, tide
      coming in, tide rising
  doing the Chinese water torture (nagging)

- What is it like to have too little water?
  dried up, withered, cut off from depths, dehydrated
  not cool
  uncleansed
  unable to reflect
  unable to receive, unable to yield, unable to surrender
  too fixed, stiff, unable to adapt, inflexible,
      rigid, unbending, thirsting

- How does water handle problems?

flow around them	dissolve them
flood them with emotion,	wear them away, erode them
drown them, drown in them	get bogged down by them

- If "wateriness" is that part of you that's about feeling, and knowing how you feel, what are some things you can do to pay attention to and nourish this part of yourself?

   establish close relationships with others, improve
      those already in existence
   let myself be poured out in service, giving
   be aware of water in my daily life, spend time near
      water, in water
   spend time with watery, feeling people

A Feeling or Water Meditation

This is a very simple way to engage one's feeling function based on the idea of "kything" (see Chapter IV). [2]

Step 1. At your centermost spot within, let all be stilled, as the waters at the bottom of a deep pool or the ocean are still even while the surface may be churning.

Step 2. Choose someone you love—or someone you would like to love better. At this deep, still spot within you, place this person. You may see his or her face or form. Perhaps you will just experience the essence of the person, that which makes him or her unique. The one you have chosen may or may not be living, and it will probably be someone you know—but it need not be. Perhaps you will choose a saint or the Lord.

Step 3. Just experience your love for the person.

Step 4. If you like, you can let this love rise up and overflow, sending it out as a prayer and blessing to the other person. Note which direction it needs to go—that is, "aim" your feeling in the actual geographic direction of the loved one. Add to it your feeling about the value you place on this person, and why that is so.

A variation:

This can be a mutual meditation with another person if you determine in advance at what time you will both practice it. Barbra Streisand sings about it: "You and I live in each other's heart."

The benefits of this meditation:

- It shows us that loving—all by itself—is something of which we are capable. Loving and being a loving person is not dependent on being loved in return. We can, like our God, love unconditionally.
- We will learn about the energizing power of loving; expressing in even such a simple way our valuing of another affects *us.*
- If we have practiced either of the centering meditations in this book that place the life of God at our physical centers (air and fire), then this sort of connecting with

a loved one unites our human loving with God's loving life in us. The two become inseparable, and loving others becomes the way to allow God's life in us to flow out. We all know this intellectually—after all, "the Bible tells us so." Experiencing it, helping it to happen in our lives, is something else.

A Reflection on Being a Water-Woman

Camping beside a running brook, the sound is always there. I go to sleep to it, wake to it. You have deep pools that I can sit in, very cold, refreshing, cleansing. By immersing myself I feel a part of you.

You sing. You are praising your Creator as you do God's will for you, happy just to be part of the creation, bringing joy and comfort, and being of use to others in whatever way you can.

Water-woman is the same: loving, caring, concerned, cleansing, forgiving, healing, aware of the deep needs of others, their hurts. I am aware of people's moods, atmosphere in a room.

I try to immerse my spirit in the spirit of water as I immerse my body in the cold brook; now I feel the stream within me, flowing from a deep Source to wherever it is sent. And it's the flowing out that really matters. Your pilgrimage from your Source to your journey's end should be a lesson for me.

I am a stream.

Fire

"Wasn't it like a fire burning in us when he talked to us . . . ?"

—Luke 24:32

Fire, like water, is a pervasive scriptural element, symbolizing everything from beginning ("let there be light") to immortality to the Holy Spirit and purification and sacrifice. Fire is about judgment and it is about the presence of God. Of all the elements, fire is the only one that needs at least one of the others to exist; it must be fed. We must be fed by the light burning within us.

These questions and answers can help us come closer to the fire in our own lives.

- What are some of the different forms fire can take?

campfire	fire on hearth	sun
electricity	fireworks	lightning
summer heat		

- What are your usual contacts with fire?

cooking	sunbathing
candlelight	lighting cigarettes

- What are some other ways people come in contact with fire (even unusual ways)?

meeting dragons	defense against wild animals
volcanoes	burning houses
tongues of fire	autumn leaves
	fire-walking, fire-eating

- What are the properties of fire?

heat	light	movement, action
radiance	consuming	reaches up
fascinating		

- When do you feel or act in fire ways that are helpful?
  warming others, "a ray of sunshine"
  when I light up (like a Christmas tree), a light
    for others, a light in the darkness, "you light
    up my life," letting light shine
  filled with enthusiasm, fired up, sparkling, radiant, filled with the Spirit
- What is it like to have too much fire?
  flaring up, boiling over, raging, hot-headed, too hot
    to handle, burned-up, volcanic, searing, scorching
  smoldering, doing a slow burn
  being flashy, blinding
  having an acid tongue
- What is it like to have too little fire?
  burned out, low in spirits, lack of energy
  gray, light covered up
  icy, unthawed, frozen, a cold fish
  no spark
- How does fire handle problems?

burn them up, overpower them, consume them
frighten them off with intensity
confront them impulsively
throw light on them

- If "fieryness" is that part of you that's about inner sparks and spirit-life, what are some things you can do to pay attention to and nourish this part of yourself?
  soak in the sun, store it up for a rainy day or winter
  consider what is spirit in me, the light Jesus asked
  us not to hide; let my light shine
  read about the human aura (or halo), learn to see auras
  burn candles, incense
  be with spirit-filled, fire people

A Spirit or Fire Meditation

You will need a lighted candle for this prayer time, and a place and time where you can sit undisturbed. This is a "baptized" version of a well-known yogic concentration technique called, in Sanskrit, *tratak.*

Step 1. Seat yourself in a comfortable position. Be sure your back won't tire; lean on something or sit in a chair if you aren't used to erect sitting postures. Place a lit candle about a yard before you, its flame at a level a little below your eyes.

Now, really adjust yourself until every part of you feels settled in place.

Step 2. When ready, begin to focus with simple attention on the flame. Let everything else—all noises in the air, other sights in the room, the thoughts of what you did yesterday or what you have to do a half hour from now—slip away to the fringes of awareness as you concentrate on the flame.

Your eyes will, at some time, close of their own accord. The flame will then be visible to you on the back of the eyelids. Continue to focus on this internal flame . . . don't think about it . . . just experience it . . . let it be. When it gets very faint, open your eyes and repeat the process. Your mind will intrude, for that is its nature. When you notice thoughts and sensations, just return calmly to the flame. Let it draw you.

Step 3. Listen to your body, and when it tells you it is ready, find the centermost place within you. From that place, reach out and draw the flame toward you in your imagination until it enters and can rest in your centerspace. Picture it there, flickering, glowing. Let it live in you. Feel its warmth at your core. See how it illuminates your whole being, then diffuses beyond your physical boundaries to envelop you and radiate outward.

Step 4. As a transition from this quiet state back to normal functioning you might feel moved to repeat or hum one of the many Scripture verses or hymn lines about light (such a line, repeated several times, makes a mantra-like chant). Among many possibilities are:

"The Lord is my light and my salvation . . ." (Ps. 27)
"Let your light shine . . ." (Mt. 5:16)
"The light of Christ has come into the world . . ." (Don Fishel)
"Light of Christ, light our way . . ." (Robert Blue)

Can you come back to these words during the day, picturing again the flame at your center?

The benefits of this meditation:

- It helps us become more aware of the fire within us, the spark of God's life at our core.
- passive meditation like this slows down all our bodily activity, calming and relaxing and refreshing us so we can function more fluently in everyday situations.
- it increases our ability to concentrate by giving us practice in harnessing the rambling, scattered nature of our minds and senses.
- it fine-tunes our sense of sight or, as William Blake put it over a hundred years ago, helps with "cleansing the doors of perception." We will have eyes that really see, much more clearly, when we return to everyday awareness from such an experience. Colors become brighter, truer, more beautiful. The smallest objects reveal their uniqueness, and people can really be seen, just as we saw them the first time.

A Reflection on Being a Fire-Woman

Fire-woman is the hardest for me to grasp and recognize in myself, because I think of fires of passion. But isn't the desire of my soul and heart to find the Source a passionate one?

I burn to grow, to be on fire. I have a burning desire to know God better, to bring God to others. I even feel like a priestess when I give out Communion.

I love to watch the rising and setting of the sun. It is our eternal source of light. I think of the light which opens the dark rooms inside and I can really relate to the unquenchable flame of faith—sometimes flaming brightly, sometimes seemingly far away and dim, but never out.

I am a flame.

A Special Day
Earth Day/Air Day/Water Day/Fire Day

"This is the day the Lord has made; let us be glad and rejoice in it."

—Psalm 117:24

You can spend a day (a week, more) with each of the elements—have your own Earth Day, for example. You might start with the element which is most natural to you, then go on to those that seem to be secondary to your nature, ending with the one most in need of developing. This is something to plan ahead of time, perhaps even sharing the day with a partner or small group. If you can collect pictures of the element in its many manifestations, put these up in advance to prime yourself. Then, on the special day, raise your consciousness of this element in your life by doing some or all of the following things. Each needs time and would make good material for an entry in your journal.

- Start by looking over the questions for the element you've chosen on the previous pages, and any answers you may have filled in. Explore these ideas more thoroughly.
- Spend some time with the element that day. Water Day, for instance, suggests a trip to a lake or river or the beach (or shooting the rapids?)—or, at least, a soak in a tub or doing lots of laundry and dishes. Earth Day could include a visit to a cemetery or a farm, or both.

  You could also go in person or in imagination to some spot where that element is in short supply. What would it be like to live *without,* say, water or fire? Or could you go somewhere where there is almost too much of the element: atop a hill where the wind makes walking difficult, for example, on Air Day?

  Immerse yourself in the element (Earth Day might be for making sand castles/mudpies) and get the physical sense of it in touch with your body, in the way of the woman who wrote the reflections.
- You might design a ritual for this point in your life that involves the element. On Earth Day one could draw a personal symbol in dirt or sand, or bury the past—written down, perhaps. Other days could feature letting go of no-longer necessary habits or attachments by burning them, casting them to the winds, or throwing them into the water. Rituals can be embellished with all sorts of things: music, readings, preparatory rites, flowers, special foods, symbolic gestures, prayer, much more.
- What memories begin to surface as you do these things? What past experiences have you had with the element? Give yourself some quiet time and space to let

both happy and painful associations surface—outdoor games as a child, vacations, perhaps old fears (of being buried or flying or drowning or being burned). What role has this element played in your life?

- Do you know any songs you can sing or play that fit the day's theme? There are lots of "sailing away" songs for Water Day, "heart on fire" songs for Fire Day, etc.
- Do some research on the element you're soaking in. What are the mythological and historical and literary and religious connections for it?

How has the Church spoken of and used earth, air, water and fire? See how many examples you can think of where the element is used in Scripture. Read some of the passages. Be there, on the scene, to watch fiery chariots ascend, or angels of the heavens descend, or water dipped from a well, or seekers travel to the promised land. The psalms, especially, are filled with nature images. Watch for examples of the elements in liturgical prayer (". . . and the heavens and the earth are full of your glory").

Native American sources can teach us a lot about the meaning in nature; a Cherokee prayer, for instance, is: "O Great Spirit, make me wise (to see . . .) the lessons you have hidden in every rock."

What movies or plays or TV programs have made good use of the element? (Remember Scarlett O'Hara's father wrapping her hand around the earth of Tara and telling her that land is the only thing that matters?)

- Who are the people in your life who personify the element you're working with? As you read Saint Barbara's story, did different people come to mind who seem to have an appropriate amount of, say, airyness? How about those with too much air? too little? and so on.

And how about relationships with these or other people—which of yours have been all sparkly, electric? which soggy, like a damp dishrag? which in the clouds and unconnected to reality, or perhaps light and breezy? which down to earth, or smothering? Focus on those suitable for the day you're celebrating.

How about your relationship to the Lord over the years? When (if ever) did it carry any of the qualities of the element you're exploring this day?

- If you have a devotion to a patron or other saint, ask if she is a good model for any one of the four women within. (Is she an earth-type saint, for instance?) Spend some time with her (or him) on the appropriate day. You could make an imaginary trip to her home for your visit. (One woman discovered four saints with her name—Elizabeth; each seemed representative of one of the four types we've been discussing.)
- Think of creatures that inhabit the element: animals, and also legendary and historical people, and figures from mythologies. Take them along with you where

you go this day (on Water Day, for instance, you might be accompanied by Noah and a few mermaids and King Neptune, as well as all sorts of creatures of the deep). Ask them what it's like to be so closely identified with their element; visit them in your imagination in the places they live.

Which figure appeals to you especially? Does she or he or it have life in you? (Is there a whale or the Little Mermaid somewhere inside, for example?) Try moving like this animal or person, or imagine yourself doing so.

- What dreams have you had that seem to be about the element of the day? Basic matter like earth, air, water and fire can have many significances; look back over your dream logs to find examples of the element. What meanings does it seem to have in your personal symbol vocabulary? How has your relationship to it changed as time passed? (One woman's dreams have shown her first being afraid of water, next venturing into it cautiously, finally happily splashing around in it.)

Maybe there is a woman (or man) in your dreams who has some strong connection to the element. If so, can you picture her in words, or draw her? Let her tell her story. Respond to it; carry on a conversation with her. Some conversations might be written down; others are better drawn in pictograms (make up your own hieroglyphics). How do you feel about her? How does she feel about you? What does she want or need? What can you learn from her?

- Draw yourself as Earth-woman, or Air-woman, or Water-woman, or Fire-woman, depending upon which is suitable for the day. Or perhaps you have a photograph of yourself that shows you as her (feeding-the-gang-at-the-family-picnic snapshots are typical Earth-woman pictures). Look again at all the language we used to describe what it was like to contain the element (just the right amount, too much, too little); what do they suggest visually in terms of *your* life?

The picture you come up with may be a composite of yourself in waking life and yourself in dream life, and may even include aspects of this woman you've learned about from other women. We are attracted to qualities we have not yet actualized in ourselves by seeing them in others (real people, fictitious heroines)—and we can learn about qualities in ourselves which aren't so great by seeing them in others and being annoyed (repelled, disgusted) by them. Put them all together to see who emerges.

Then, really get to know this "woman within"; her strengths and weaknesses, her likes and dislikes, how she feels, how she acts, what brings her out, what sends her into hiding, what she wants, even what clothes she wears. Does she have a name? If this part of you is just emerging, you might also like to come up with a vision of what you hope she will become. What could help her flower?

This isn't an easy exercise, especially when you are "out of your element." It needs thought, and time (the rest of your life), and prayer. If drawing the Earth-woman (etc.) is too much of a task, perhaps you can find pictures to cut out that, put together, will at least be close to what you think and feel and sense and intuit about this person within. Or you can settle for describing her with secondary symbols (words, that is).

- Spend time with the meditation designed for each element, perhaps even having someone read it for you, guiding you along. Or you could record it on tape ahead of time. Two of the meditations (earth and fire) are what are called "passive meditations," needing time set aside for them; two (air and water) are "active" or "walking meditations," ones which can be done while you go about your other activities. These might be combined with, say, jogging, or swimming, while the sitting or passive meditations might deserve a special place set up just for this time.

- Set aside some even simpler prayer time at the end of the day. In stillness, get the feel of yourself filled with earth or air or water or fire—not too much, not too little, just enough. Let all the day's experiences be part of you. Give this as much time as it needs.

- Is there some way you can carry over your raised consciousness of the element you've been working on today to the rest of your days? For example, if earth is the element, what activity do you perform daily that is earth-ness for you? It might be house-cleaning or getting up at night with the baby, or it might be that chunk of the day when you give kind attention to your own body. Can you somehow remind yourself to let that time also be a time of awareness of the earth-woman in you?

The point is to preserve the fruits of these experiences and let the nature of each element soak in, become a permanent part of you. Reading about them doesn't do this; going through experiences with them does.

The Elements Combined

". . . and you must put on the new self which is created in God's likeness."
—Ephesians 4:24

We have played with the elements separately up until now, just as we explored them separately in Barbara's story. Of course, they aren't so neatly divided in nature or in our souls; the alchemists spoke of the *prima materia* or confused mass of material which had to be separated before its parts could be transformed and reunited into the pure "gold" that was their goal. (Remember that we spoke of the alchemists attempting to do with matter what we are really called to do psychospiritually. Actually the *prima materia* was not so much a definite substance as a concept for an initial psychological situation of confusion and lack of clarity.[3]) Earlier the Greeks had spoken of the coming together of the elements into something greater than any of them, the *quinta essentia* or quintessence or ether. In the East, the assembled energies of the universe are known as the life force, or *prana* or *chi* or *ki.*

The discrimination of the parts of the whole is a necessary step. The goal, however, is the union of these ingredients into a new creation. Our story, like Barbara's, ends in new life. Here are some ideas to help the symbols we've been using be brought together. Staying with them a while longer may raise our consciousness of what that new person we are called to become is like.

- As each element becomes more clearly defined in you, it can interact more clearly with the others. Here are some ways to create this sort of dialogue.

  What happens, say, when fire and water in you come together? Do you get the sense of the fire being quenched? or does the water turn to steam as the fire overpowers it? (You almost have to feel this kinesthetically.) If air meets earth in you, what sort of conversation do they have? Or, better, how does the encounter feel? Can these elements support each other—or are they so different that they cancel each other out? Try all the combinations to come up with some ideas on which elements need to be restrained, which need to be strengthened and encouraged, which are functioning as assets to you and which are deficits.

  If you have access to a copy of the ancient Chinese book of wisdom, the *I Ching,* you can see that it contains sixty-four hexagrams composed of pairs of "people." There are four women, one for each of the elements (earth, wind, lake and fire) and four corresponding men (mountain, heaven, water, thunder). The combinations that ensue when two of these are juxtaposed (or when one is doubled) give what the Chinese thought to be the totality of possible outer and inner life situations. Fire under the lake, for instance, results in the hexagram for Revolution, Changing, while lake under the fire is about Opposition and Contradiction. If you feel yourself to be one or two of these eight "people" in an especially strong way, you might look up the hexagrams containing them. Do they speak to you of your own life? How? (The *I Ching* speaks in generalities; it is designed to hook what we already know at a deep, unformulated level and bring it to the surface via projection, not to be used as a divination tool or parlor game.)

- Is there some sort of activity you can engage in that involves all four elements? Pottery making—a beautifully scriptural activity—is one:

  Earth, formless, is taken from nature and turned in on itself. This wedging, as it is called, is a rough and painful process, but a necessary one if the pot is to be strong. Centered on the potter's wheel, the mass has water added to it—not too much, lest it fall apart; not too little, or it will not be pliable. The pot grows at its own pace, and when in shape is put in the air to dry—again, just the right amount of air. Then it is fired, and if it is well-made, it will survive even intense heat and live forever.[4]

- Find a passage from Scripture that has all four elements in it (one is John 21:1–19, the fish breakfast after the resurrection). Be there, savor it slowly, getting the feel of the earth in the scene, the other elements—and how real each of these was to the people of the Bible. Our sense of Scripture is strongly colored by our understanding of how precious the soil of the Holy Land was (and still is) to her people, how the heavens above this land spoke of the divine to them, how valued the small amount of water was, how fiery the sun is in the Near East. The four elements we have been working with are omnipresent in biblical life.

- Did you make pictures of yourself as each of the four women within? Make a mandala of them, in a circle around the center point of a cross. (If you are using the correlations we have used in this book, earth and fire are opposite each other; air and water are the second pair of opposites.) Is the whole, somehow, greater than the sum of all its parts? Perhaps you have one female figure who seems to be all four of these inner women rolled into one. She can go in the center. Rejoice if you have met her!

  Perhaps you even came up with a present version of these women and also a future, potential version of each (the women you hope will be you someday). This will give you material for two mandalas: one about what is, one about what might be.

  Designs like this are most effective when put up where they can be seen. They trigger a lot of inner activity. What do these women say to you? to each other? to any inner men?

- Spend some quiet time visualizing and praying about the uniting in you of the forces we've been exploring. Is there a place you can do this that puts you in contact with all four elements—the beach, for instance? or indoors, by an open window where the sun and air come in, surrounded by growing things, a cup of tea in hand?

  Be with the earth and air and water and fire. Really feel them physically, outside and then within. Let them mingle together, as your body becomes a melting pot for their essences—and for the bonding of them with that which is "Other." (We can use our *physical* experience of the body as enclosed vessel—or "bridal chamber"—as a teacher about the *psychospiritual* experiences described in

Chapter 6. It is important, too, to remember that though we can prepare ourselves for the gift of increasing consciousness, we are not the Giver of it.[5])

A Prayer

Giver of life, here I am in the midst of all your gifts. I feel the earth under me, holy ground. The air blows by me, through me. The waters keep rolling in, never stopping—they speak to me of deepening. And the sun filtering down seems to circle me with sparks of your Spirit.

May I become more amd more aware of the splendor of these ordinary things. May these gifts of yours come together within me, as they do without. Let them transform each other, transform me.

What I do here is, I know, important—but who I am is what matters even more. May your gifts lead to new life flowing through me as they did for your handmaid Barbara, so long ago, so far away.

I am a vessel.

(See footnote 5. on page 91 for explanation of art.)

1. For further food for thought on the elements both in our lives and in history, see *Maps of Consciousness* by Ralph Metzner (New York: Collier Books, 1971), Chapter 4, and *Astrology, Psychology and the Four Elements* by Stephen Arroyo (Davis, CA: CRCS Publications, 1975). The latter book gives a great deal of history on the universal use of the four elements to describe aspects of the soul.

2. Thanks to Louis M. Savary and Patricia Berne for making the kything ideas better known.

3. See the fascinating "Psychotherapy and Alchemy," especially the introductory article in *Quadrant,* Volume II, No. 1, Summer 1978, and subsequent chapters in following issues of the New York Jung Institute's journal: author, Edward Edinger.

4. Thanks to Bannie Giovanetti for her pottery experiences. See also *Centering* by Mary Richards (Middletown, CT: Wesleyan University Press, 1962).

5. A symbolic parallel to this meditative experience comes from the medieval world of the alchemists, whose vessels in which raw materials—the elements, that is—were transformed were the same sort of container. And sometimes, the alchemical vessel was shaped like a tower, just as happened in Barbara's story. (See *Psychology and Alchemy,* p. 3.)

Symbols of the Feminine

"Behold the handmaid of the Lord; be it done unto me according to thy word."
—Luke 1:38

How can we ever hope to describe the gentle power that enables us to be receptive and, therefore, in relationship—to ourselves, to others, to our environment, to our God? We can try to explain it with words, words like

- non-active, incoming, static, resting, non-striving, stillness, waiting, taking time, contemplative
- indirectness, diffuseness, winding, allowing, yielding, surrendering, letting go
- practicality, grounding, collecting, connectedness, relationship, receptivity, containing, gathering, embracing, enclosing, nurturing, loving, beauty, subjectivity, accepting ambiguity, not needing to understand, going beyond/around logic, welcoming
- mixing, merging, unifying, synthesizing, community, family
- listening, absorbing, non-linear, simultaneous, waning, solid, acausal, essence-oriented, caring for what is already present

or just
- being.

The sages do better, speaking of the feminine energy in the universe in ways such as these

"Mary kept all these things carefully in her heart and pondered them . . ."
—Luke 2:19

"Without going outside, you may know the whole world. . . .The farther you go, the less you know."
—Tao Te Ching

"Watch, therefore, for you know neither the day nor the hour . . ."
—Matthew 25:13

Symbols of the Masculine

"I will rise and I will go about the city; in the streets and the broad ways I will seek him whom my soul loveth."

—Canticles 3:2

The masculine, the great creative force in the universe . . . do we dare try to harness it with letters and phrases? Those who do come up with words like

- active, outgoing, dynamic, moving, initiating, making things happen, assertion, achieving
- directness, straightforwardness, focus, single-pointedness, definiteness
- theorizing, analysis, probing, taking apart, abstraction, objectivity, needing to understand, logic
- separating, discriminating, order, structure, individuality, naming
- expressing, telling, linear, sequential, waxing, volatile, causal, process-oriented, going on to something new

or just

- doing.

But, as might be expected, the poets capture the masculine energy more accurately. They say

"Ask, and you will receive; seek, and you will find; knock and the door will be opened to you."

—Matthew 7:7

"Rise, my soul, and stretch thy wings, thy better portion trace,
Rise from transitory things t'ward heaven, thy native place;
Sun and moon and stars decay, time shall soon this earth remove,
Rise my soul, and haste away to seats prepared above."

—American folk hymn, words by Robert Seagrave (1693–1759?)

Feminine

Most eloquent are the symbols of the feminine which have arisen spontaneously from peoples of all times and places, tellingly alike from age to age.* Some of these are:

the night: time of resting and stillness and surrender to sleep. Therefore, the qualities and images associated with night time:
- *darkness, shadows, shade,* even autumn and winter, the darkening times of year.
- *coolness,* which soothes and congeals (but too much becomes paralyzing cold).
- *the moon*—with its cycles and changing size, so closely linked to women's physiology. The moon is a reflecting heavenly body; it needs to receive in order to give light. Furthermore, it doesn't have an independent life of its own, as the sun (viewed from earth) seems to; the moon is a satellite, home-based around one planet, mirroring the feminine quality of connectedness. With its monthly rather than daily cycle the moon has always seemed the more contemplative and non-striving of the heavenly lights. Francis of Assisi called the moon "Sister" in his famous *Canticle to the Sun.*
- *silver*—the color of the moon and other night-time luminaries (stars, comets).

earth and water: the two elements particularly associated with the feminine, because they reach downward and take in and unify in ways that air and fire do not. They are also slower moving, like the moon and the less active feminine principle. Water, especially, in the form of *curling waves* and *wandering streams,* has seemed to many peoples to speak of the indirectness associated with the *yin* energy. To Francis, these elements were "Sister Water" and "Sister Mother Earth."

curving, sinuous shapes and things: like so many water formations, including *harbors* and *bays* and *seaports* that welcome men home from the high seas. The *sea* itself is often spoken of as feminine. The *crescent moon,* especially, has this curved cradle shape. Among animals, *cats* and *cows* with their soft lines have long been considered feminine animals. And on land, *small hills* and *mounds* match this type of flow in the universe.

---

*While these images are found to have almost universal similarity, there are always exceptions; the moon, for instance, has been a symbol of the masculine in isolated instances.

Masculine

Again, it is the symbols of the masculine which best tell us what this force is like. Some of the most universal are:

the day: time of newness, the time when things can be seen so they can be acted upon, named, studied. Therefore, the qualities and images associated with day time:
- *light,* and *spring* and *summer* as times of new and longer light.
- *warmth,* which produces fruitfulness (but too much scorches and roasts).
- *the sun*—which seems to be born again each morning, which obviously (to the ancients) had a mind of its own as it inexorably moved on its journey across the sky. The daily cycle of the sun, when compared with the four-week cycle of the moon, gave it a more aggressive "personality." It was, to Saint Francis, "honored Brother Sun."
- *gold*—the color of the sun.

fire and air: the two elements particularly associated with the masculine, because they reach upward toward the heavens. Like the sun, they are active, moving at a higher vibratory rate than earth and water. Fire, especially (the element of the sun), in the form of *lights, candles, torches* and *lightning,* is connected with the masculine. Francis, very at home with the traditional genders assigned to the elements, addresses both fire and wind as "Brother."

upright, straight shapes and things: *straight lines,* especially vertical lines that head heavenward; *staircases, ladders,* * *roads,* the whole idea of *traveling; mountains* that seem to touch the sky, and their man-made counterparts—the *pyramids* and *ziggurats; pillars, columns, cylinders; arrows* that can aim straight and far. Among animals, those that are known for strength and for direct movement: *the goat, the ram, the horse, the bull. Clubs, scepters, swords.*

---

*Matthew Fox does an interesting comparison of (Jacob's) ladder spirituality and (Sarah's) circle of spiritual growth in Chapter 2 of *Compassion* (Minneapolis: Winston Press, Inc., 1979).

matter, the body, the land: the practical, down-to-earth side of daily living. And, for this reason, the *horizontal* (like the cross-bar of the cross). Also *chronological time,* as measured by clocks and calendars.

enclosed spaces: which take one in, places like *caves, homes, enclosed gardens,* one's own *room, walled cities, Noah's ark,* all *ships* (traditionally referred to as "she") including *space ships, sanctuaries, wells, groves of trees.* And also, enclosed spaces which not only contain but pour out: *vessels, vases, pitchers, baskets, bowls, cups, eggs, shells.* And *labyrinths, trenches.* Also, things that enclose by framing: *doorways, windows, picture frames, horseshoes* and, most of all, *circles.*

open things: that show the receptive nature—an *open hand,* an *open flower* (the rose, the peony and the lily being traditional feminine flowers because of their shapes as well as their great beauty).

fruitful plants and animals: these speak of the productivity that is the result of receiving and nourishing: *rabbits, doves, the pomegranate, trees laden with fruit, shrubs and gardens in bloom.*

Of course, many of these symbols have other associations as well as the feminine. And many have specific Judaeo-Christian implications that post-date their origins as images of the feminine. These symbols may show up in dreams; they form the basis of hundreds of legends and fairy tales and songs. Living with one or just a few of them can help us experience more fully the beautiful resting and welcoming energy of the feminine principle as it meanders through our lives.

Masculine

spirit, heaven, the sky: the non-material side of life. *Eternal time.*

creation images: the *potter,* anyone or anything that begins something new, is self-starting: *dawn, the first star* (light in the darkness), *new fire* (such as that kindled from flint in the Easter Vigil). Things that emerge, such as *sprouts* coming from the ground, *butterflies* coming from cocoons, the *phoenix* resurrected; *new pelts* on animals, *new skins* on snakes. Also, *order-out-of-chaos images*—subduing a dragon, taming a wild bull or horse, bullfighting and slaying the bull, earth taking shape out of formlessness and desolation.

things divided into parts: *patchwork quilts, puzzles, boxes* with lots of separations in them, *maps* and *charts,* anything with pieces that fit together; the *alphabet.*

moving things: a swiftly flowing *river,* a *tornado* or *hurricane, trains, cars, planes;* animals noted for their swiftness: the *hare,* hastening toward heaven, *the stag.* Birds, because of their ability to move swiftly, and also because they inhabit the air, from which they can look down and see all the patterns.

There are many more images of the masculine energy in us and in the whole of creation. The reader will note that a few of these have attached themselves very strongly to Jesus (the sun, light, gold, the scepter)—but they also pre-date the Christian era. Jesus carries them for us because he is, for so many, the ultimate human incarnation of the masculine principle. (He is also connected with some feminine images, such as the egg at Easter. Jesus is an example, a wonderful example, of one who marries masculine and feminine in his being. Mary, androgynous also, has not only feminine symbols but also some of the masculine attributes; for example, we say she is a "woman clothed with the sun.") When we spend time with even one of these *yang*-like images and its manifestations in our life, we deepen our experience of the active, creative principle which is such a necessary part of us all.

Symbols of Union

"You will be like a beautiful crown for the Lord. . . .No longer will . . . your land be called 'Desolate' . . . (it) will be called 'Happily Married.' "

—Isaiah 62:4

We are surrounded by the interplay of the two opposite flows in the universe. These complements confront each other in our souls, in the natural world in which we move, in our encounters with others, in the cosmic dance. They may war . . . or be in occasional dialogue . . . or, best of all, unite to support and cover each other lovingly.

Down through the centuries, this conjunction of masculine and feminine (which mirrors the greater conjunction of the soul and its God) has been envisioned in many ways—in words

". . . God created human beings, making them to be like himself. He created them male and female, blessed them, and said, 'Have many children. . . .' "

—Genesis 1:27–28

"The one was buried in Mary's kirk, the other in Mary's choir,
Out of her breast sprang a red, red rose, and out of his a briar.
They grew and grew to the old church top, till they could grow no higher,
And there they tied in a true lover's knot, the rose twined round the briar."

—floating Anglo-American ballad verse

and, far better, in the symbol of

marriage: the word picture of Jesus, Isaiah, Hosea, the Song of Songs, as well as many other scriptures of various religions and early peoples. Sometimes *the bride and bridegroom* are a royal couple: *the king and the queen, the prince and the princess.* Sometimes they are *the sun and the moon being wed,* a Tantric image seen today as a transparency on the backs of car windows. These are called *hieros gamos* symbols, a phrase meaning the union of heaven and earth (or masculine and feminine).

There are other representations of the marriage, not as explicitly male and female as are the bride and groom:

- *the Star of David*—its two triangles denoting heaven (the pointing-downward triangle) and earth (the pointing-upward triangle).
- *the tree,* especially the sacred trees of so many cultures—its branches reach up to the heavens, its roots dive deep down into the earth.
- *the astrological signs of Gemini and Capricorn and Sagittarius*—when Gemini is shown as a brother and sister pair of twins, it is an image of male and female in

harmony; Capricorn is the dolphin-goat, whose curling tail reaches down into the waters and whose goat-nature impels him or her up the rocky cliffs; Sagittarius is tied to the ground by his centaur's body, but he aims for the skies with his bow and arrow.

- *the cross*—vertical upreach joined to horizontal leveling and stabilizing, a pre-Christian symbol in use long before the time of Jesus, who fulfills its meaning. A cross with its four arms the same length (the Greek cross) depicts this union of opposites best.
- *the whole brain*—its left hemisphere represents analytical thought, its right the ability to combine; together they stand for the uniting of these two complements.
- *the T'ai Chi*—the ancient Chinese circle which holds both the light *yang* shape and the dark *yin* shape, each with a dot of the other at its core.
- *head and heart united*—a very common, if somewhat simplistic way of describing the coming together of the two partners. Throughout the centuries this has been depicted by pairs of persons who represent each: Aristotle and Plato, the Greek gods Apollo and Dionysius, even the Odd Couple!
- *the homecoming theme*—either the wandering hero who returns to his beloved (like Ulysses), or the wandering people who return to their beloved motherland (the Israelites). In both examples, the masculine energy, which has been moving and going out, comes back to unite with the feminine, which has stood still. Dorothy returns to Kansas, which has always been there; the Apollo space vessels return to mother earth; the prodigal son returns to his home—and on and on throughout the pages of history and literature.
- *the mythical unicorn*—the unicorn's twisted horn is really a coming together of polarities in him; he is an androgynous animal. Because of his white coat, standing for purity, and the ease with which the unicorn was supposedly vulnerable to wounding, he has often been associated with Jesus. He is shown many times in medieval art in the care of the Virgin or a lady in her set-apart garden space. This makes the unicorn a double marriage image, reminding us of both the lesser and greater inner marriages to which we are called.
- *the rainbow*—joining the heavens and the earth.

There are other representations of the coming together of heaven and earth in us—images like precious stones, and mandala images, separate places complete unto themselves (like islands and the garden of Paradise) and the fourfold circle or square we've discussed at length earlier—but it is these images of marriage that best express the love involved in the inner unitings. Spirit-saturated matter and matter-saturated spirit coming together, neither pretending it does not need the other, nor that there is no difference between them—their marriage produces new life, the new creation that is our potentiality. We might choose just one of the above symbols to live with at a time, asking it to speak to us of wedding. The reader may have sensed, just on reading the above, the power of these numinous images. There are none more able to stir us up; they deserve to be treated with great wonder.

Four-ness

". . . I saw four angels standing at the four corners of the earth, holding back the four winds . . ."

—Revelation 7:1

As we noted in Saint Barbara's story, the number four—or, more specifically, the pattern of fourfoldness—has long represented totality. According to the theory of correspondences, analogous patterns appear and reappear because of the unity of all creation. That is, what is true for the tiniest atom is true in pattern for humans and also for the galaxy. Whether or not one accepts this as a scientific paradigm, it makes interesting speculation to see how C. G. Jung's typology (the functions of thinking, feeling, sensation and intuition, which he also augmented by speaking of the two attitudes of introversion and extraversion) "fits" with other systems of fours. Some of these are:

- the four humors of medieval times, body fluids that supposedly gave rise to four types of personalities: sanguine, phlegmatic, choleric and melancholic.
- four long-lasting schools of Christian spirituality, the Benedictine being very earth- or sensation-oriented, the Dominican based on *Veritas* or the search for truth (primarily through study), the Franciscan definitely being a feeling spirituality, and the mystical Carmelite school of Teresa and John loaded with leaps of intuitive faith (and fire imagery, for that matter).
- four yogas from the Hindu tradition, each about linking the person to God: the *bhakti yoga* tradition being about feeling and devotion, *karma yoga* being about work and body and sensation, *jnani yoga* based on intellectual expansion, and *rajah yoga* ("the yoga of kings") being the meditative tradition that sees around corners—or, in another vocabulary, is intuitive.

More important than this sort of research, however, is whether or not fourfoldness seems to have a home in us.* To test this out, here is

---

*The reader is referred back to Chapter II, notes 4 and 5, for further references and qualifications about this theory. See also the indexed references to the motif of four in *Man and His Symbols.*

A Final Experiment

Keep a small log of foursomes, or quarternities, in your life, past as well as present. Jot them down, or—better still—draw them. Here are some places to look for them:

Your outer environment—look around your home, the place where you work, the special places in your community that have always attracted you. Reminisce about childhood places. There will be fourfold designs and groups of people and patterns in abundance, even in as simple places as rug and wallpaper designs and clock faces.

Your inner life—go over old dreams, noting images of four (or multiples of four: eight, twelve, forty, four hundred, etc.); these may appear as pairs of people, or square shapes, or book titles or in any number of ways. What symbols with fourfoldness have been part of your life for years (the cross, a favorite flower perhaps)? What symbols do you find yourself drawn to now that repeat this pattern?

Collecting these potent images in one place and just living with them is a way of speaking to yourself about the wholeness four is said to represent. The fact that this number in its visual forms has appeared throughout history and all around the globe to represent totality is no accident. We can let it continue to speak to us and work in us today.

How Symbols Work

I T MAY BE HELPFUL, as a final postscript to Barbara's story and our stories, to
take another brief look at what we've been about. Understanding the theory
behind experiences is helpful.

We've been soaking ourselves in what are sometimes called "transformation
symbols," images so basic and universal and powerful that living with them helps
with the transformation of a person into the born-again new creation of which Jesus
and Paul told us. Each of these transforming symbols can stand, as we have seen, for
a certain type of energy. The energy can flow smoothly in us, or be repressed (too
little available to us), or be uncontrolled (too much).

More and more our understanding of *energy* seems to be the common
denominator that unites such diverse disciplines as quantum physics, the ancient
religions, depth psychology, holistic health and healing, new age education
(especially the application of the left and right brain research and the holography
studies), the martial arts, and several others. The frontier study being done in each
of these fields is resulting in their being brought together under this umbrella of
energy and energy transmutation. It isn't that we mean to reduce, for example,
Christianity and the action of the Spirit to *nothing but* energy manifestation. Of
course not. The energy studies, rather, give us a language which is understandable
to people of many different lights and backgrounds, a common vocabulary to speak
about inner/religious experience.[1]

So, by sensitizing ourselves to the energy flow that a particular symbol has *for us* (and it may be about something different for another person), we connect ourselves up to a deep inner level that pre-dates words. Symbols like those in Barbara's story point beyond themselves, mediating another reality to us as another language does. They work in us, open up doors. And they have a healing function as well, bringing together the disparate and wounded parts of us into that harmonious whole which is the unique person dreamed of by God since the beginning of time.

A transformation symbol cannot be created, is never quite able to be pinned down, and certainly should not be dissected. When we get too specific about naming symbols and finding pat meanings for them, we strip them of their vitality and their ability to function as transmitters. We make them remote and distant. This trivializes them; Mircea Eliade, the famous historian of religions, warns us of the "degradation of the symbol." Trying to circumscribe the powerful symbols sent to us by our dreaming life and our waking life is our human way of clutching at them, desiring them. When this happens, we are less able to experience the pre-verbal, numinous level to which a symbol points. We need a "take off your shoes" attitude of reverence toward the might the transformation symbols represent for us. This caution is equally true in connection with ritual—or enacted symbol. The ritual (whether it be grand liturgy or home tradition) that is too analyzed, too understood, loses its power. It becomes something "out there" rather than something "in here."[2]

So, again, the reader is encouraged to find the power symbols that are hers, let them do their catalytic fermenting in her, live with them, play with them, pray with them, enjoy them, stand in awe of them. We live in a time when the tools of transformation (symbols being one of these tools) and the knowledge of how to go from unformed, unconscious being to fullest personhood are available to everyone. This is new! Until just a few decades ago, the sort of personal transformation we've been exploring was thought to be the province of the specially blessed, those who were showered with "extra" grace to become saints. But we have all always been that full of grace, and we have long had the vision of letting it shine forth. Now we also have much more practical know-how about human potentiality—and this is what all the optimistic talk of a new age is about, despite the agonizing problems of our world. We *are* standing on the threshold of a dream.

1. Three very helpful works exploring energy within and without are *Psychic Energy* by M. Esther Harding (Princeton: Princeton University Press, 1947), *The Ultimate Athlete* by George Leonard (New York: Viking Press, 1974) and *Joy's Way* by W. Brugh Joy (Los Angeles: J. P. Tarcher, Inc., 1979). They give us very similar material from the viewpoints of analytical psychology, the revisioning of sports and the body (based on the martial arts), and transformational healing, respectively.

Those who are at home with Teilhard's cryptology will recognize his "noodynamic viewpoint" as being a Christian version of the energy-as-unifying-principle-of-all-experience stance. See his wrestlings with the topic, for instance, in *The Phenomenon of Man* (New York: Harper and Row, 1959) and *Human Energy* (New York: Harcourt, Brace and World, 1979; originally published 1972). George Maloney's writings also help us see this harmonizing of the Christian tradition with the others mentioned; see, among others of his works, *Inscape: God at the Heart of Matter* (Denville, NJ: Dimension Books, 1978).

The reader who has the picture of the studies on energy—physical, psychical, spiritual, cosmic, all sorts—being the blanket or umbrella will find many ways to use this unifying framework for all sorts of previously unrelated information and experience. An especially useful overview of new age thought that integrates the many disciplines we've mentioned is *The Aquarian Conspiracy: Personal and Social Transformation in the 1980's* by Marilyn Ferguson, editor of the *Brain/Mind Bulletin* (Los Angeles: J. P. Tarcher, 1980).

2. There are volumes written on symbols and how they work in us. Some of the most useful references the reader may want to explore are *Psychosynthesis* by Roberto Assagioli, "the Italian Jung" (New York: The Viking Press, 1965); Erich Fromm's *The Forgotten Language* (New York: Holt, Rinehart and Winston, 1951); *Stages of Faith* by James Fowler (New York: Harper and Row, 1981), which gives us information on a developmental stage theory that shows how our symbol appreciation evolves as faith grows—and vice versa (see also *Life Maps* by James Fowler and Sam Keen [Waco, TX: Word, Inc., 1978]); Chapter 5 of *The Feminine* by Ann Bedford Ulanov, titled "The Symbol and Theology" (Evanston: Northwestern University Press, 1971); and, more abstrusely, Volume 5 of the *Collected Works* of C. G. Jung, *Symbols of Transformation* (Princeton: Princeton University Press, rev. ed., 1952), and Volume 18, miscellaneous writings gathered under the blanket title of *The Symbolic Life* (Princeton: Princeton University Press, 1976). See also Dr. Edinger's *Ego and Archetype,* which has several rich selections on symbols in our lives, and fallacious relationships to them (see especially pp. 107ff on "The Search for Meaning").